Designing
Mediation

APPROACHES TO TRAINING AND PRACTICE
WITHIN A TRANSFORMATIVE FRAMEWORK

Edited by

Joseph P. Folger

Robert A. Baruch Bush

Published by

The Institute for the Study of Conflict Transformation

CONTENTS

INTRODUCTION

Our original goals in writing *The Promise of Mediation* were twofold. We wanted to offer a clear conceptual framework for understanding how mediation could be practiced within a transformative framework. We knew that many practitioners valued this approach to conflict intervention and had been practicing this way since the inception of the alternative dispute resolution movement. But we also knew that the theoretical framework that underlies this approach to practice was not well articulated and was not at the heart of many standard mediation training programs. Many trainings stem from very different premises and result in a very different form of practice. As a result, our second goal was to lay the foundation for moving the transformative framework into a more central place in mediation practice.

Since the publication of *The Promise of Mediation* we have been able to make important strides in the development of transformative practice. This is largely due to the good fortune of working with many admired colleagues – excellent trainers and practitioners – who are committed to the development of this framework and are highly skilled at articulating it. Over the past five years, we have worked with our colleagues in designing and delivering numerous trainings for mediation programs and individual practitioners who wanted to keep or place the processes of empowerment and recognition at the heart of their work. Collectively, we have learned a great deal from working on these trainings. The purpose of this volume is to share some of what we have learned in doing this work – to offer the insights that have emerged through the development of these training initiatives.

The articles in this volume will be helpful to those who want to develop training in the transformative approach in whatever arena of practice they work. We believe that there should not be one design for mediation training within this framework but many different approaches to instruction that are based on the same underlying premises and orientation. For this reason, this volume is not a training manual. The articles are intended to be thought-pro-

1

voking pieces that can stimulate the development of training designs. The articles offer examples of training materials and exercises but these illustrations are not intended as prescriptions for training agendas. Rather, they are meant to encourage others to create new (and even better) ways to bring across the fundamentals of this approach to practice. We hope that this book enables many practitioners and trainers to develop their own training designs based on the processes of empowerment and recognition that are discussed in *The Promise of Mediation.*

This book is also intended for practitioners who want to learn more about the "inner workings" of transformative practice, apart from the way it is taught in training. Many of the articles help to illustrate how mediators can practice within this framework – what it means to work with opportunities for empowerment and recognition, to follow the parties and to avoid intentional or inadvertent directiveness in practice. The articles make clear why the transformative approach to practice is different from standard problem-solving practice. They clarify how this approach to practice can allow for a transformation of the parties' conflict interaction.

Overview of the Chapters

The book is divided into three sections. The first section, "Theory: Understanding the Framework," focuses on the underlying premises that define the transformative approach to mediation. Training programs are the primary events where mediation theory gets translated into the "how-to" of practice. The design and content of trainings reflect what people think mediation should be. The articles in this section discuss the importance of examining not just the "how" of practice but the "why." The authors address a range of questions including: What is the purpose of practice in a transformative framework? Why are mediators being taught a particular set of skills? To what end should these skills be put? How can one tell whether any given skill is being used to serve the goals of a transformative process?

In this section, Beal and Saul's piece "Examining Assumptions: Training Mediators for Transformative Practice" clarifies the relational premises behind the transformative approach to practice and discusses what these premises mean for mediation practice. The authors rely heavily on their own experience in training mediators and offer a set of steps that can be taken to help practitioners who want to adopt a transformative orientation in their work.

This first section also includes a reprint of Folger and Bush's (1996) article "Transformative Mediation and Third Party Intervention: Ten Hallmarks of a Transformative Approach to Practice." This article summarizes the important practice commitments that mediators make when they practice

2

within a transformative framework. It captures some of the "rules" mediators follow when their goals center on supporting processes of empowerment and recognition.

Charbonneau's article, "How Practical is Theory" addresses why it is important to include theory in mediation training and offers useful insights about how to integrate theory into training designs. Charbonneau sees trainers as "disturbers of the peace" – they are there to help create doubt about the premises one might hold, and to enable practitioners to move to transformative approaches to practice that might challenge long held beliefs or inclinations.

In "Myths and Misconceptions about the Transformative Orientation," Della Noce, Bush and Folger point to some of the most common misunderstandings about the transformative approach. These misunderstandings and myths often need to be clarified in training because they clarify how mediators can be sidetracked if they do not understand the underlying framework for this approach to practice.

Folger clarifies the inevitable link between the content of a dispute and the process that is followed in addressing it. In his article, "Who Owns What in Mediation?: Seeing the Link Between Process and Content," Folger demonstrates why it is important for parties to own both process and content elements during their mediations and why this approach is at the core of transformative practice.

Pope and Bush's article, "Understanding Conflict and Human Capacity: The Role of Premises in Mediation Training" addresses the underlying premises of the model from a training perspective. They illustrate how sample exercises used in training reflect the underlying assumptions of the transformative model.

The second section, "Transformative Mediation Training: Tools for Instruction," offers a series of articles that discuss specific methods, models and exercises that can be used in training to help convey the nature of transformative practice. These articles provide numerous examples of activities that have worked well in trainings to teach a range of conceptual and communication skills that are central to transformative interventions. These pieces also offer ways of conceptualizing the process as a whole and illustrations of how mediators work as the moment-to-moment interaction unfolds in a mediation session.

In the chapter entitled "Mediation as a Transformative Process: Insights on Structure and Movement," Della Noce explains why the standard stage models of the mediation process, that picture the mediation process as a set series of chronological phases, are not consistent with the transformative approach to practice. She offers an alternative, cyclical model that places party decision making at the heart of the process and captures the way in which empowerment and recognition unfold incrementally and interdependently.

In her article on "Beginning the Mediation: Party Participation Promotes Empowerment and Recognition," Pope rethinks the mediator's "opening statement" in a session from a transformative framework, noting the many opportunities for empowerment that unfold at this very early stage of the process. She describes how to conduct an "opening conversation" with the parties that describes the goals, nature of the process, role of the mediator, etc., in line with underlying transformative premises.

Della Noce's chapter, "Recognition in Theory, Practice and Training," clarifies the role of recognition in transformative practice. She distinguishes between instrumental empathy - a concern within traditional, individualistic approaches to practice, and relational empathy - an end in itself in transformative practice. This distinction is important in clarifying the very different ways in which problem-solving and transformative mediation see the role of recognition in productive conflict.

The last two articles in this section of the book are an interrelated set focusing on how mediators can work moment-to-moment with opportunities for empowerment and recognition as a session unfolds. Moen et al.'s chapter, "Identifying Opportunities for Empowerment and Recognition in Mediation," provides a close analysis of conflict interaction to help clarify what opportunities for empowerment and recognition look like. This analysis is key in understanding how mediators can identify these opportunities as parties speak and interact during a mediation session. This article also categorizes empowerment and recognition opportunities in ways that are particularly useful in supporting mediators' ability to focus on the micro-opportunities that arise in the interaction.

In "Microfocusing in Mediation: The What and How of Transformative Opportunities" Jorgensen et al. describe the range of ways mediators can respond to opportunities for empowerment and recognition after they arise at any moment in a mediation session. These responses allow mediators to support decision-making of all kinds for the parties and to support inter-party recognition if that is consistent with the parties' inclinations. Taken together, these last two articles offer a foundation for training mediators' "micro-skills" - the ability to focus on the here and now of the parties' interaction and to be proactive in helping the parties work with opportunities for empowerment and recognition as they arise.

In the final section of the book, "Training Within a Transformative Framework," two articles address issues of training methodology – how training is conducted and what principles should guide an instructor's goals and styles of interaction with the training participants. Stains' chapter, "Reflective

Training: Matching Educational Practice with Transformative Intention," considers the role of the trainer as a transformative practitioner. He examines the commitments that trainers make when they design and deliver a training seminar on the same principles as the transformative approach to mediation being taught. Stains clarifies that, "[a]n effective learning environment provides a space where practitioners reconnect with their own transformative experiences, feel the effects of empowerment and recognition and come to understand what they can do to encourage or inhibit those qualities in themselves and others."

Finally, in "Developing Transformative Training: A View from the Inside," Folger and Bush draw on their experience in developing both beginning and advanced mediation trainings to present several training principles that can act as guideposts for those designing and delivering training within the transformative framework. They discuss some of the complications and pitfalls of conducting training and ways to overcome obstacles that trainees often face in learning the approach.

Acknowledgments

We would like to express our sincere appreciation to the William and Flora Hewlett Foundation and the Surdna Foundation for funding several key training development and assessment projects that have built the foundation for many of the ideas in this volume. The generosity of these foundations has made much of the developmental work on transformative training possible.

We would also like to thank those who participated in or sponsored many of the trainings over the past five years. Specifically, we would like to thank all of the participants in the Training Design Project – those who gave their insights in the think-tank weekends and those who developed materials and designs for training in the transformative approach. We also owe a great deal to those who initiated and conducted the transformative mediation program for the United States Postal Service REDRESS™ program. Our appreciation goes first to Cindy Hallberlin who launched this important and ground-breaking program. We also want to thank Dorothy Della Noce and Sally Pope for their many contributions to the design of the USPS training as well as the trainers who helped roll out this program. Their feedback on the training has been most helpful in carrying the design to a new level of instructional excellence.

We are also grateful to Patricia Gonsalves, at Greenwich Mediation Center, whose creative fund raising abilities and foresight enabled her Center to support an introductory training for volunteer mediators. She created a wonderful training opportunity that served as an instructional laboratory for us to think through the best ways to train new mediators within this approach to practice.

We would like to thank all of the contributors to this volume. It has been our great pleasure to get to know insightful and creative people over the past several years and to have the opportunity to learn from their many training and practitioner insights. Their articles contribute greatly to the advancement of not only training, but also the transformative model itself. And finally, we sincerely appreciate the excellent contributions Ross Brinkert made in developing and producing the manuscript for publication.

PART I

Theory:

Understanding the Transformative Framework

ONE

Examining Assumptions:
Training Mediators for Transformative Practice

By Susan Beal & Judith A. Saul

Getting Started

Like many mediators, we learned to mediate in what we now recognize as a facilitative, problem-solving framework. We were taught the structure of the mediation process and the listening and negotiation skills that we would use to move parties from positions to interests, and then hopefully to agreement. We began training mediators, improving upon what we learned but maintaining the basic components of structure and skills. We were careful to emphasize that parties were responsible for the content of a mediation. But mediators were experts in process, and we taught that our control of process was central to what we did.

As we continued to practice mediation and teach mediators, we realized that most mediators equated success with agreement. The temptation to become directive was great, often rationalized by the desire to "help" parties "succeed." Skillful mediators realized the power of the facilitator: by controlling process, they affected outcome. The clear distinction between process and content began to blur.

When we first read *The Promise of Mediation*, we were reminded of what had originally drawn us to mediation, a process that allowed people to make decisions for themselves. Bush and Folger's clear articulation of premises, for both transformative mediation and problem-solving mediation, rang true. We were struck by the ways in which our training and practice had slipped from the ideals that led us to become mediators. We decided to step back and take a critical look at what we were doing. Once we began that journey, we realized that transformative mediation required significant changes to both our practice and our training.

Our goal was to practice in ways consistent with the premises we believed in and to create training for beginning and experienced mediators

9

that incorporated exercises and theory supporting a transformative approach to practice. As we gained experience with this practice, we realized that our training would have to move away from a reliance on the structure of the mediation process. **Instead, mediators would need to understand the basic principles of transformative practice and the benefits of mediating within this as opposed to other frameworks. This understanding would allow them to choose whether or not to embrace this form of practice, a decision which we believed would be based in large part on whether its premises were consistent with theirs.**

The Premises of Transformative Mediation

While some mediators have criticized Bush and Folger for clearly stating underlying assumptions, claiming that their own work is value free, we believe that mediators, like parties in a conflict, are not working in a vacuum. They are affected by the values and beliefs that make up their worldview as well as by their own reactions to conflict. Since all practice is based on a set of premises, articulating these premises and helping mediators understand the relationship between purpose and practice is an important part of preparing mediators to work with parties in conflict. Bush and Folger's clear articulation of premises places skills and techniques within a framework that help us compare and assess different forms of practice.

Stated most simply, the worldview that Bush and Folger posit as central to the practice of transformative mediation is relational: people are interconnected. Each of us has a separate identity, but we exist in relation to others. **Acknowledging the truth of our interconnectedness leads us to balance our own desire for autonomy and self-fulfillment with our need to connect with others, who have similar and sometimes competing needs.** Success in balancing these competing needs results in a position of **compassionate strength**, that is, the ability to be strong in self yet responsive to others. Rather than acting out of self-interest, aiming for the satisfaction of personal needs and desires (a premise of the problem-solving model), people balance the inevitable tension between advancing their own needs and allowing or assisting others to meet theirs.

Transformative mediation also recognizes each person's individuality and their capacity to make decisions for themselves. Transformative mediators accept the fact that they cannot understand others' situations, especially given the limited interaction they have during a mediation. Thus they avoid the role of advice-giver, focusing instead on assisting parties in gaining clarity. Similarly, they accept that people are capable of making decisions for themselves, whether or not mediators understand or agree with a particular decision.

10

In addition to these premises about people and their capabilities, Bush and Folger articulate premises about conflict. They state that the problem-solving model assumes that conflict is the result of an obstacle in the way of an individual meeting his/her need. This reflects the individualistic world-view that dominates mainstream American culture, a culture infused with a competitive ideology. The quality of the relationship between people in conflict becomes secondary to the satisfaction of individual needs. Problem-solving mediators facilitate negotiation between people whose needs appear incompatible, ideally helping parties move from positions to interests and then to agreement.

In contrast, Bush and Folger see conflict as a crisis in human interaction. In their view, conflict often causes people to close down and become suspicious, defensive and mistrustful. The specific problem to be resolved gets covered by layers of emotion and assumptions. People lose perspective, lack clarity about what is going on and are less open to the needs of others. They experience a diminished ability to communicate and make good decisions.

Given conflict's effect on people's capacities, responding to conflict from a transformative standpoint is about more than rationally solving a problem. It is about listening, clearing up confusion and opening up to new information. It is about empowerment, providing a chance for people to become more fully aware of their own strengths, resources and options. It is also about recognition, helping people to consider and perhaps respond to the needs of others. As mediators focus on opportunities for empowerment and recognition, parties in a conflict are better able to realize their inherent capacity to make good decisions and solve problems. **Thus another premise of transformative mediation is that conflict provides the opportunity to learn to act from strength instead of weakness, compassion instead of selfishness.**

In both *The Promise of Mediation* and their later essay, "The Ten Hallmarks of Transformative Practice," Bush and Folger describe behaviors and techniques of mediators practicing within a transformative framework. **However, these behaviors and techniques are less central to transformative practice than the values and attitudes that influence them.** For example, in "The Ten Hallmarks of Transformative Practice," mediators are advised to develop:

- "conscious awareness, control and suspension of judgment"
- "a sense of humility that makes it easier to refrain from exercising judgment"
- "[an assumption of] the parties' underlying competence and decency"
- "an awareness of their own attitudes and assumptions about the parties"

11

- "[the ability to] allow and encourage parties to express their feelings"
- "comfort with ambiguity"
- "the attitude of acceptance and calmness about the limits and vicissitudes of intervention"

This emphasis on attitude dovetailed with our own experience training and working with hundreds of mediators during the last fifteen years. The many stylistic differences we have observed mattered less than an attitude of calmness, optimism and comfort with conflict, attitudes related to the belief that conflict provides an opportunity for parties to grow in self-knowledge and respect for others. Transformative mediators respect parties and their choices and are patient with whatever pace the parties set, attitudes related to the belief that parties "have what it takes." In these ways, premises - the "why" behind any behavior or technique - relate directly to the choices mediators make: purpose drives practice.

A Changed Role for the Mediator

Mediators who reflect on their premises and choose to practice within a transformative framework find that their role changes as well. Problem-solving mediation, the kind most mediators were trained in, puts the mediator firmly in control of the process. It has built-in safeguards: carefully constructed stages, ground rules, turn-taking, and a focus on the future. These procedural guidelines act as regulators. They render the mediation process less vulnerable to the effects of both mediators' and parties' personalities and their reactions to conflict. They also allay mediators' fears by allowing them to maintain control.

Mediators practicing within a transformative framework, however, are asked to dispense with many of these practices and replace them with an orientation and a role very different from that of the problem-solving mediator. In this fluid process, mediators are asked to trust that the parties "have what it takes," that they know the most about their situation, and that they are better able to judge the value of possible solutions or no solution. **Rather than directing the parties through the process, transformative mediators invite parties to shape process as well as content.** Mediators are present, in the moment, following the parties as they move through their conflict journey. Rather than focusing on issues to be resolved, transformative mediators highlight opportunities for empowerment and recognition. They move at the parties' pace, comfortable with expressions of conflict, emotion, confusion and ambiguity. Transformative mediators watch for and are satisfied with small steps, realizing that they are "stepping into a stream of interaction" rather than directing and completing an isolated transaction.

The transformative framework requires that the process as well as the content of mediation be responsive to the parties and that mediators be relaxed and non-judgmental. It requires letting go of the fear of losing control and of the need for a solution or agreement as a sign of our success. To do this, mediators need to be self-reflective. They need to understand the beliefs that guide them and the ways in which they react to conflict so they are not controlled by those reactions.

Resisting Self-Reflection

It is the rare mediation training that asks mediators to explore their underlying beliefs and values as part of learning to mediate. This is unfortunate, because examining one's assumptions, prejudices, and fears is a critical first step to understanding ingrained, often unhelpful responses to conflict. These responses limit our ability to respond to others with openness, compassion and trust. The safeguards built into the process of problem solving mediation generally provide enough structure for mediators to maintain control and manage the conflict of others, whether or not they have considered their own attitudes toward conflict and their underlying view of human interactions.

Most of us resist examining, or even admitting to, our own fears, weaknesses and prejudices. We find it much easier to encourage other people to work through their fears and their conflict rather than examine our own. Mediating within a problem-solving framework allows us to focus on the parties' reactions and behaviors, and what we should or shouldn't do to favorably influence those reactions, behaviors and the outcome of the mediation.

A clear example of this desire to keep the focus off ourselves came from an in-service designed to help mediators examine their personal fears and assumptions brought up by a difficult mediation. We were attempting to help our problem-solving mediators build self-knowledge so they could consider mediating in more transformative ways. We explained that we were setting up a situation that might test the limits of their (problem solving) skills. The issues in the role-play scenario were fairly straightforward: two men, in business together, were having trouble agreeing on the future direction of that business. However, the characters each had difficult personalities. One would repeatedly challenge the mediators' authority and expertise. The other would take every opportunity to lecture on his strong religious beliefs. We warned our mediators that the challenge might lie in the beliefs and behaviors of the parties, rather than the issues.

We set up the role-play with rotating mediators. One after another, the mediators foundered. There was animated discussion on the sidelines about what to try, and in spite of the various techniques they tried, mediators constantly found themselves stuck. Some were stopped by the unpleasantness of having their role challenged. Others had trouble managing their distaste for one party's strong religious opinions. Reactions varied. Some mediators became very directive, sharply limiting the time parties were allowed to talk, steering the topics of discussion toward "safe" issues and away from "problematic" ones. Other mediators took offense and got caught up in arguments with the parties. One mediator responded by cracking jokes and insulting the parties. Another froze up and found it difficult to speak. Some withdrew or became vague, prompting even more impatience on the part of the parties.

In the discussion that followed the role-play, mediators were asked to describe what it had felt like to face such difficult parties. Despite many different interventions, few mediators felt good about what they had done. Perhaps most interestingly, **in nearly every case, the mediators described the problem as lying with the parties for not responding well to mediation.** When asked what they felt while facing such a challenge and finding themselves drawn into the conflict, the mediators again responded by describing the behaviors that they had found difficult. The mediators were reminded that the point of the in-service was to focus attention not on the parties, but on themselves and their reactions. Even so, they found it difficult to discuss the fears that had been brought up by the mediation.

When the discussion did turn to the anger, frustration, and discouragement most mediators had experienced, they finally acknowledged that what lay under those feelings was fear: fear of incompetence, fear of increased conflict, and fear of failure. After much discussion, the mediators acknowledged that because they could not control the interaction or turn it into one they found acceptable, they were at a loss and did not know what to do.

Before we finished the discussion, we asked those who played the parties to talk about what was going on for them. They shared the mediators' frustrations. They felt stuck in their conflict and manipulated by the mediators' attempts to move them to places they didn't want to go. They found themselves fighting with the mediators in addition to each other.

We then invited mediators to reflect with us on the limits of the problem-solving process. We explained that in contrast to problem-solving mediation, transformative mediation does not expect the mediator to control the process but to trust the parties enough to follow them through their conflict, while highlighting opportunities for empowerment and recognition. They agreed that they had failed in their goal of controlling the conflict and getting agreement on the issues. We could only speculate on what might have happened if they had focused instead on providing opportunities for the parties to understand their options and resources and reflect on each other's perspectives. We encouraged them to consider changing the focus of their attention from issues and agreement to opportunities for empowerment and recognition. We suggested that they might have been more effective if their focus had been on facilitating the parties' communication rather than controlling it.

This example is one of many we could describe which illustrate the difficulty of getting mediators to deal with their fear of losing control and their lack of faith in people to resolve their own disputes. Yet without examining their premises and fears, how could their practice be consistent with the framework of transformative mediation? **The looser structure, the larger role played by the parties themselves and the increased conflict and emotion accepted within the session remove from the mediators the safety of being "in control."** The impulse to be directive in a mediation often arises from either the fear of things being out of control or the sense that "the mediator knows best." Thus a mediator who is familiar with the rugged terrain of his or her own assumptions about parties' competence and about conflict will be more confident when accompanying parties through their conflict.

Incorporating Premises into Training

The centrality of premises and the not atypical difficulty we faced in encouraging mediators to confront their lack of faith in the parties and their fears about conflict led us to change our training. We have begun to experiment with different ways of engaging both new and experienced mediators in these important components of mediation training. Our repertoire of exercises has been enriched by ideas we have borrowed from others who share our goal of training mediators to work within a transformative framework. We find our most successful attempts involve introspection, reflection on personal experiences with conflict and new experiences that challenge assumptions.

One of our first changes was incorporating techniques to increase "psychic readiness" into our training. We realized that mediators would be unable to focus on parties and their interactions if they were thinking about their own issues. So we talk with mediators about how they can prepare for mediation by sitting quietly for a few moments, gathering their thoughts, letting go of the busy-ness of the rest of their day and clearing their minds in preparation for the task at hand. We encourage them to engage in an open and honest conversation with their co-mediator about their emotional state, their sense of readiness and what they hope to learn as they mediate. This is modeled in all of the simulations we do and is practiced by trainees during role-plays.

A newer series of exercises asks mediators to reflect on their beliefs about conflict and the attitudes related to those beliefs. Several of these exercises include nonverbal activities. We ask mediators to select a color they associate with conflict and talk about their selection. Colors chosen most often relate to the strong emotion and "heat" associated with conflict. We show a video clip of people in intense verbal conflict and ask mediators to note their physical and physiological responses to what they see and hear. We ask them to reflect on the messages they received about conflict through their families and their cultures and how these messages affect their responses.

We sometimes ask mediators to draw a picture of themselves in a tough conflict they faced. Those willing are asked to talk about what they've drawn. People often portray themselves as small compared to others, backed into a corner, under a cloud or weighed down by a heavy object. These drawings dramatically illustrate the sense of weakness that often accompanies conflict. Other times we ask people to draw a picture of an animal they'd choose to take with them if they had an appointment with conflict and the quality that animal represents. Animals frequently chosen include a lion (ferocity), an owl (wisdom), a gorilla (strength), a rhinoceros (protection), and even a teddy bear (safety). People's choices again illustrate the fear and weakness they feel.

The discussion that follows each of these exercises builds self-knowledge in mediators, as well as empathy for those with whom they will work. The self-knowledge gained makes mediators more comfortable with the conflict that happens in the course of mediation. As they share their widely varied responses, they grow to appreciate the different ways people respond to conflict. This in turn makes mediators more sensitive to what they might otherwise miss or misinterpret.

We invite mediators to share their personal experiences with conflict. We put people in pairs and ask them to tell a story about a conflict. The other then listens in several different ways: silently, actively (reflecting feelings and summarizing content) and as an expert helper (offering advice or suggestions). Listeners realize how hard it is to "just listen." Speakers talk about the way it felt to be listened to in the different ways. Most agree that getting advice was less valuable than the self-knowledge that resulted when they received high-quality attention free of judgment.

A related exercise asks a person to talk about a situation they face where they are unsure about what to do. The listener is instructed to listen actively, without giving advice or making suggestions. After switching roles, the group discusses the effect of "just" being listened to. People often describe how valuable it was to "just get it off my chest," to be able to speak without being interrupted or challenged. They often note with surprise that when they heard themselves talking, they realized that they had the answer in themselves. Others report that just describing their options out loud helped them gain clarity. This powerful exercise helps mediators appreciate the value of active listening, of staying in the moment with the parties, trusting that they will gain clarity and move toward the answers that are right for them.

In another exercise we ask people to think about a tough conflict of their own, present or past. Half of the group reflects on what made it hard to resolve, half on what helped resolve it. We chart people's responses, with the almost-universal result that the interpersonal dynamics are the toughest part of conflict: "it's the disputing; not the dispute." This exercise clarifies the value of a mediator focusing on the parties' interactions, since those are what most often make conflicts difficult to resolve.

We ask people to talk with us about trusting others. What gets in the way of trusting people's ability to resolve their own conflicts? How do they feel about giving advice? How do they respond to getting advice? When is it welcome and useful? When does it anger or shake self-confidence? All of this opens mediators up to treating parties in conflict as most of us would like to be treated, as competent people able to decide what is best for ourselves.

We give mediators a maze and ask them to find the way through. After a minute or two, we ask them to turn to those sitting nearby and compare solutions. They discover that there were many paths to the end. When we ask people to describe how they tackled the maze, they find that various strategies yielded successful results. We then talk about the lessons in the maze for us as mediators. Comments frequently include: people start in very different places; different paths all get to the same place; there's not one right answer; if you get stuck, you can back up and try again. The exercise reinforces the value of party choice, since the mediator's way to tackle an issue may not be the way that works best for the parties.

As we engage mediators in these exercises and conversations, we bring them back to the premises upon which transformative mediation is built. We encourage them to consider their willingness and ability to mediate based on these premises. We remind them that choice is central for mediators as well as for parties. As this model becomes better known, the decision about whether or not to mediate within a transformative framework is a choice that each mediator must make.

We continue to develop and gather exercises that promote self-reflection because of the importance of self-knowledge and the need to consciously accept the premises to practice transformative mediation. **Mediators need to take time to ask themselves what they really believe about conflict, about the way the world works, about human nature.** We suspect that unless these premises are already part of their worldview, mediators are likely to run into conflicts between what they believe, on the inside, and what they practice, on the outside. Such a clash between personal beliefs and the premises upon which transformative mediation is founded is likely to lead in one of two directions. Mediators either become directive in their mediation or they become confused and sloppy as they try to slavishly reproduce behaviors that they neither understand nor have integrated.

Conclusion

We are experimenting with the placement of these exercises in our basic mediation training and are using many of them in workshops for experienced mediators. We now understand that skill training, however effective, is insufficient. To adequately prepare mediators, we need to focus (or re-focus) on three levels:

- **Premises or Worldview** - the beliefs, values and assumptions through which we make sense of the world, and which sustain the attitudes that inform our practice of mediation.
- **Emotional self-awareness and control** - the personal feelings that influence our reactions to events and relationships, and that can either enhance or hinder our effectiveness as mediators.
- **Skills and techniques** - the tools we use as mediators.

These three components build on each other. There is value in all mediators understanding the relationship of premises to practice and in gaining self-awareness, whatever framework they choose to mediate within. But premises and attitudes are especially critical to the transformative framework since they are the "why" behind any particular mediator action, its purpose, which determines its effectiveness in providing opportunities for party empowerment and recognition.

We realize that mediating within a transformative framework involves a leap of faith. Trusting others does not come easily to many of us. It is a process, not something that happens at once. As practitioners of transformative mediation, we have gained greater appreciation of the theory. As trainers, we have learned a great deal by listening to others discuss these premises and their implications for practice. We do our best to help others gain clarity, in part by welcoming the confusion and accepting the resistance that often accompanies grappling with new ideas. We respect the need for people to make their own choices.

In closing, we will simply say that it has been, and continues to be a fascinating and humbling experience, attempting to incorporate a more transformative approach not only into our training, but also into our own mediation practice. **We are struck by the parallel between the need for an open and trusting attitude within mediation, and the need for the same**

openness and trust in training. As with mediation, we realize that we are not the "expert" trainers, designing a model that will turn out perfect transformative mediators. Instead, we are involved in a process of learning, adapting, and remaining open to the successes and challenges that are part of the process. Balancing our desire to be responsive to the individuals within a training, with the need to impart a large amount of information and skill in a limited number of hours, all within a transformative framework, feels at times like trying to rein in three horses running in different directions. Yet we believe that the attitudes and worldview—the quality of "compassionate strength"—contained within the transformative approach, are not just for mediation, but for every relationship. We would like to see the world operate more like a transformative mediation. We'll start by training mediators.

TWO

Transformative Mediation and Third Party Intervention: Ten Hallmarks of Transformative Mediation Practice

By Joseph P. Folger & Robert A. Baruch Bush

The Transformative Framework: Moving from Theory to Practice

In programs offering training in the transformative approach to media-tion, we often begin by asking practicing mediators to describe one of their most highly successful mediation sessions. Almost without exception, the mediators find this an easy task - and the stories they tell share a common theme. Almost all the mediators describe sessions in which something hap-pened that produced visible changes in the way the parties related to their own situations and to each other, such as:

> "One of the parties, who was hopelessly confused at the outset, gradually became crystal clear about what she needed and how she might get it. The change was astonishing."

> "One party, who had obviously never been able to speak up to the other party before, seemed to 'find his voice', and made some very effective statements and arguments that opened everyone's eyes."

> "The parties came in as 'sworn enemies', reluctant even to talk to one anoth-er. Then at some point they began to relate differently to each other, and then started talking freely and even joking with each other. By the end of the session, there was an amazing difference."

These and other stories offer vivid illustrations of difficult situations where the parties clarified what was at issue for them and what they wanted to do about it, while, at the same time, reaching a greater understanding of the other's perspective or life situation. In effect, the "success stories" that they tell attest to the fact that, for many mediators, the transformative effects of the process are what make it most meaningful and successful.

At a conceptual level, the transformative approach to third party practice is based on certain premises about both the effects and the dynamics of intervention. One major premise of the approach is that processes like mediation have the potential to generate transformative effects, and that these effects are highly valuable both for the parties and for society (Bush and Folger, 1994). Specifically, mediation's potential transformative effects are that it can strengthen people's capacity to analyze situations and make effective decisions for themselves, and it can strengthen people's capacity to see and consider the perspectives of others. In short, mediation is a process that enables people in conflict to develop a greater degree of both self-determination and responsiveness to others, while they explore solutions to specific issues. However - and this is the second major premise of the approach - mediation is likely to have these transformative effects only to the extent that mediators develop a mindset, and habits of practice, that concentrate on the opportunities that arise during the process for party *empowerment* and inter-party *recognition*.

A focus on empowerment means that the mediator watches for the points in the process where parties have opportunities to gain greater clarity about their goals, resources, options, and preferences - and then works with these opportunities to support the parties' own process of making clear and deliberate decisions. A focus on recognition means that the third party watches for those points where disputants face the choice of how much consideration to give the perspective, views, or experiences of the other - and then works to support the parties' own decision making and perspective-taking efforts at these points. It is in this sense that mediation is potentially transformative: it offers individuals the opportunity to strengthen and integrate their capacities for self-determination and responsiveness to others. If these effects are seen as valuable, the transformative approach to practice will make sense at the conceptual level.

The key question that arises in implementing the transformative approach is how to move from this theoretical and conceptual framework to the practice level. For example, in training programs we have presented, mediators often express great interest in the transformative model; but they are unsure whether what they typically do in practice is consistent with, or fully expresses, a non-settlement driven, transformative approach. When we ask them what they did as mediators that contributed to their successful mediations (in continuing the "illustrations of success" exercise) their responses are very revealing. Most mediators say that the parties did it themselves: the disputants were simply "ready", and they themselves did very little, as mediators, to contribute to the successes they had described. However, when we begin to ask the mediators specific follow-up questions about their moves - questions designed to find out whether they had done the kinds of things that a mediator committed to the transformative approach might do - the mediators' responses change. They indicate that they actually made many of the "transformative" moves that we asked about. And they realize that they had more to do with the direction and results of these "successful" sessions than they first thought.

The lesson that emerges is that, even when mediators are attracted to the transformative approach conceptually and intuitively, they may not be able to identify the specific strategies that implement this approach at the practice level - or even recognize these strategies at work in their own practice. In looking for ways to translate the transformative framework more completely into the vocabulary of practice, we started asking experienced mediators (including ourselves) questions like the following: If you were observing yourselves - on videotape, for example - in the sessions that turned out to have transformative effects, what kinds of patterns would you expect to see in your own mediator behaviors? If you wanted to assess whether mediators in a program you administered were committed to a transformative approach to practice, how would you assess this? What would you be looking for in observing their interventions, and what questions might you ask them about their commitments to practice?

This practice-centered inquiry helped to identify a set of indicators, or "hallmarks," of a transformative approach to practice. These hallmarks constitute key habits or patterns of practice that, when evident in a mediator's work, signal his or her commitment to a transformative approach to intervention. While not reaching the level of detail that direct coaching in the transformative approach might provide, they certainly advance the effort to translate the transformative framework into practice terms. They do so by describing the typical responses that flow from this framework, to a number of practice issues that mediators face on a regular basis.

For example, imagine a session in which one party gives a very confused and rambling opening statement. Then, in a first caucus called by the mediator to help clarify things, the party continues to "wander around" from issue to issue, point to point, without any clear direction. At every move by the mediator to pursue one point or issue, or summarize, the party moves in a different direction. What kind(s) of responses to this situation would show that the mediator employs a transformative approach to practice? Is there a "hallmark" response that flows from the transformative framework when put into practice, and shows the mediator is following it? Our goal is to provide some answers to questions like these.

In this article, we first identify and discuss ten hallmarks of a transformative approach to practice. We then explain how an awareness of these practice habits or commitments can be useful in advancing a clear understanding of the transformative vision of practice. Finally, we suggest that there are a number of conflict intervention arenas where forms of third party practice are emerging that are consistent with this approach.

Ten Hallmarks of Transformative Practice

We suggest that when mediators are effectively putting the transformative approach into practice, the ten patterns or habits of practice discussed below will be evident in their work. In the terms used above, these kinds of practices are some of the hallmarks of the transformative approach to mediation. Each of the ten points describes, in part, what the work of a mediator implementing the transformative framework "looks like", and what attitudes and mindset she or he carries into practice. In considering each of these points, mediators interested in the transformative approach can ask themselves: If I watched myself practicing, would I see myself consistently following these habits of practice? If asked about the mindset and premises that my practice is based on, would I respond with the kind of statements that introduce (and summarize) the points described below?

1. "The Opening Statement Says It All": Describing the Mediator's Role and Objectives in Terms Based on Empowerment and Recognition.

Mediators and other third parties following a transformative approach begin their interventions with a clear statement that their objective is to create a context which will allow and help the parties to: (a) clarify their own goals, resources, options, preferences, and make clear decisions for themselves about their situation; and (b) consider and better understand the perspective of the other party, *if* they decide they want to do so.

The mediator devotes some significant time and effort to explaining this third party role, not assuming that it will be understood automatically. The mediator emphasizes that she is not there to make decisions for the parties, or to pressure them to come to some conclusion or agreement if they are not ready to. In some form or other, the mediator conveys to the parties that the goal of the process is to allow them to understand the situation - and each other - better and to help them decide, what, if anything, they want to do about the issue or problem that they face.

In orienting the parties about what a "successful" session might achieve, the intervenor frames formal agreement or settlement as one possible outcome of the process. However, instead of adopting a one-dimensional focus on settlement as the only aim of the process, the opening statement describes other outcomes that can be equally important. It emphasizes that the session can be successful if new insights are reached, if choices are clarified, or if new understandings of each other's views are achieved. The parties are encouraged to see any of these as positive outcomes and important accomplishments of the process, as significant as specific terms of agreement or action plans that may be reached.

As a rough "test" of whether an intervenor's work includes this habit of practice, the following questions might be asked: Do the opening statements they make regularly include reference to anything *other* than agreement (on some or all issues) as the goal of the process and definition of "success"? If so, are "non-agreement" goals and potential outcomes of mediation described with clarity, and placed on a par with settlement, in a way that gives the parties a sense of their real value? Positive answers suggest that the transformative framework is being carried through into practice.

2. "It's Ultimately the Parties' Choice": Leaving Responsibility for Outcome With the Parties.

If third parties feel a sense of responsibility for "producing" certain outcomes in their interventions, they are unlikely to be practicing within the transformative framework. An important hallmark of the transformative approach is that its practitioners consciously reject feelings of responsibility for generating agreements, solving the parties' problem, healing the parties, or bringing about reconciliation between them. Instead, third parties following a transformative framework sensitize themselves to *feeling responsible for setting a context for, and supporting, the parties' own efforts* at deliberation, decision-making, communication and perspective-taking.

Thus, the mediator feels a keen sense of responsibility for recognizing and calling attention to opportunities for empowerment and recognition that might be missed by the parties themselves, and for helping the parties to take advantage of these opportunities as they see fit. In practice, calling attention to these opportunities means inviting the parties to slow down and consider the implications or questions that follow from a statement one of them has made. A few simple examples: To frame and help capture an opportunity for empowerment, the mediator may follow up an unclear statement from one party about goals or options by saying, "I'm not sure I understand fully what you've said; can you talk a bit more about that?" The party's ensuing restatement, and perhaps further questions, may produce a greater level of clarity and empowerment. Likewise, to frame and capture an opportunity for recognition, the mediator might call one party's attention to a statement the other has offered to explain their past conduct, and then ask the listening party whether the information contained in the statement might alter her view of the other disputant or the conflict in general.

However, in identifying and working with such opportunities for empowerment and recognition, the mediator remains clear that all decisions about *how to respond* to these opportunities are the parties' own, and rejects any feeling of responsibility for the decisions thus made. When a mediator begins to feel that he is responsible for ensuring a certain outcome - whether achieving an agreement among the parties, altering their views of one another, or creating change of any kind in the parties or their situation - this feeling will in all likelihood lead the mediator into directive and disempowering steps that negate the transformative dimensions of the process.

When he firmly grasps the transformative framework, the mediator recognizes and feels strongly that *only the choices or changes that the parties freely make,* regarding what to do about their situation or how they see each other, will be of real or lasting value. This strong conviction allows - and actually impels - the intervenor to refuse to take over responsibility from the parties for the key decisions to be made about how their conflict interaction unfolds and what its outcome will be. This commitment to place and keep responsibility for the conflict firmly in the parties' hands is a hallmark of transformative practice.

3. "The Parties Know Best": Consciously Refusing to Be Judgmental about the Parties' Views and Decisions.

Another commitment of transformative practice - related to but distinct from the one just described - involves the refusal to be judgmental about the parties' views and decisions about their situation and each other. The value placed on empowerment within the transformative framework motivates third parties who follow this approach to consciously avoid exercising judgment about the parties' views, options and choices.

This does not (and cannot) mean that the mediator somehow "does away with" personal values or viewpoints. However, the mediator develops the ability both to recognize her own judgmental feelings when they arise, and then to pull back and suspend judgment instead of exercising it. Thus, the mediator "catches" herself quickly if she begins to feel, "I understand the parties' problem better than they do," or "I know what would be the best thing for the parties to do here". And, having caught these judgmental feelings, the mediator then consciously "steps away from" her own judgment and refuses to exercise it to influence the parties' views and choices.

In addition to refraining from actually exercising judgment, the mediator is careful not to let parties "read things into" her statements or actions. Thus,

25

when suggesting options or "reality testing", these moves are conducted in a self-consciously provisional manner - putting ideas on the floor for the parties to consider, but without conveying any sense that the mediator will be disappointed or displeased if the parties do not respond in a favored direction.

Conscious awareness, control and suspension of judgment is thus a clear hallmark of transformative practice. The mediator is helped in this habit of practice by another kind of awareness that also flows from the transformative framework. That is, the mediator constantly remains aware that, no matter how much information is revealed, she actually knows very little for sure about the parties, their situation, and their lives as a whole - and immeasurably less than the parties themselves. This conscious awareness of her relative "ignorance" creates a sense of humility that makes it easier to refrain from exercising judgment, and especially from overriding the parties' judgment.

One important "test" of a mediator's commitment to this hallmark of practice is the way the mediator responds when there seems to be a clear power advantage on one side. In this situation, it is easy for third parties to feel a need to defend and assist the apparently weaker party. However, this feeling involves judgments and assumptions on several levels: that the power balance is in fact what it seems to be, though power relations are often complex and multi-layered; that the "powerful" party is being strategic or conniving, though they may actually be uncertain of how to act and relying on power patterns that they themselves would prefer to change; or that the "weaker" party *wants* a shift in the power balance, though they may prefer the current situation for reasons unknown to the intervenor. Any or all of these judgments, and the "power balancing" strategies that they justify, lead to third party moves that quickly negate empowerment in the transformative sense.

A commitment to transformative practice leads mediators to a different kind of response to apparent power imbalances. The mediator understands that shifts in power can certainly occur within a transformative approach, but she does not presume to prompt such shifts. Instead of exercising independent judgment about the power balance, the mediator is guided by the party's judgment. The mediator looks for, and inquires about, signals from a disputant that he is troubled by an imbalance or is unable to sustain a viable position without some change in the power balance. If and when such dissatisfaction is expressed, the mediator helps the disputant to clarify exactly what he wants, to convey what he wants to express to the other party, and to make the decisions that then arise. However, if a seemingly weaker party gives no signals of need when he appears to be overrun by a stronger disputant, then for the mediator to push the imbalance issue substitutes her judgment for the party's, and moves toward a highly directive intervenor role inconsistent with the transformative approach.

The sign of transformative practice is that the third party's actions are *responsive* to the disputants' moves - because it is the party's judgment that controls. A shift of power is not an outcome prompted or justified by third-party judgment; rather, it is one possible result of a series of moves that the parties themselves initiate, based on their own judgments.

4. "The Parties Have What it Takes": Taking an Optimistic View of Parties' Competence and Motives.

The previous hallmark involved not being judgmental about the parties' views and decisions about their situation and each other. This one involves not being judgmental about *the parties themselves* and their character. How a third party thinks about the disputants themselves - in particular, whether he is basically optimistic or pessimistic about the parties' abilities and motives - is a strong indicator of whether or not he is carrying the transformative framework into actual practice. Third parties who successfully implement a transformative approach are consistently positive in their view of the disputants' fundamental competence - their ability to deal with their own situation on their own terms. Likewise, they take a positive view of the disputants' motives - the good faith and decency that underlies their behavior in the conflict situation, whatever the appearances may be. In short, taking an optimistic view of the parties' inherent competence and motives is a hallmark of transformative practice.

To frame the point differently, the mediator does not base his view of the disputants on immediate appearances. The mediator sees the disputants - even in their worst moments - as being only *temporarily* disabled, weakened, defensive or self-absorbed. He is convinced that, while the conflict may be causing the parties to be alienated from themselves and each other, it has not destroyed their fundamental ability to move - with assistance, but of their own volition - from weakness to strength or from self-absorption to recognition of others. In social psychological terms, third parties who follow a transformative approach to practice avoid the "fundamental attribution error" (Jones and Davis, 1965; Kelley, 1971) - they do not attribute the parties' difficulty in finding their way through the conflict to their "bad character" as inherently weak, hateful, or uncaring people. Rather, they attribute the parties' ineffective behavior to the circumstantial effects of the experience of conflict itself.

This commitment to assuming the disputants' underlying competence and decency is actually quite critical to a transformative approach, because it directly affects the steps the mediator will and will not take in practice. If a mediator believes that the parties are incapable of making good decisions about how to deal with their situation, he will be drawn to take over responsibility and act directively, instead of supporting the parties' own decision-making. Likewise, if a mediator believes that the parties are driven by purely selfish motives, there is little reason to invite them to consider each other's perspectives, since neither will want to (and if they did, it would confirm their worst suspicions!). The assumption of competency motivates the mediator to reject the feeling that disputants are essentially dependent on him, and instead allow them to determine their own outcome. The assumption of decency motivates the mediator to show the parties opportunities for recognition that he would otherwise think it pointless to bring up.

Maintaining an optimistic view of the parties' capabilities does not mean that transformative mediators are oblivious to behavior that might be labeled destructive or in bad faith. However, the real question is: What does a mediator *do* when a disputant engages in behavior that the mediator feels is ill-intentioned and destructive? Like the response outlined in the previous section, describing how mediators can respond to perceived power imbalances, transformative practitioners take their lead here from the reactions of the parties themselves. When one party states or implies that the other may be acting in bad faith or undermining the process, the mediator allows, encourages and helps the concerned party to safely pursue this concern to his or her satisfaction. If and when that party is satisfied, the process can continue; or, if this concern cannot be worked out, the party may choose to leave the mediation. However, the mediator does not step forward with his own judgment of bad faith, or "decision to terminate", without some prompting expression of concern from a disputant. Making unprompted judgment calls and decisions about the bad motives or effects of a disputant's moves or reactions is a clear departure from the non-directive and empowering role that transformative mediators are committed to.

To test for this hallmark of transformative practice (beyond examining their response to the type of situation discussed in the preceding paragraph), intervenors can simply focus their awareness on their own attitudes and assumptions about the parties in cases they are handling - when the intervention begins, during, and after. If honestly done, this very private "test" of the attitudes and assumptions we hold about our clients can reveal some quite surprising results.

5. "There Are Facts in the Feelings": Allowing and Being Responsive to Parties' Expression of Emotions.

In transformative practice, third parties view the expression of emotion - anger, hurt, frustration, etc. - as an integral part of the conflict process.

Intervenors therefore expect and allow the parties to express emotions, and they are prepared to work with these expressions of emotion as the conflict unfolds.

This practice grows, not out of an attempt to serve therapeutic goals, but out of an attempt to reach transformative ones - since the expression of emotion often indicates important opportunities for empowerment and recognition. Frustration, for example, is often the emotional expression of troubling uncertainty about what, if anything, will be a workable course of action, or what choices a party has available to him or her. In other words, frustration often signals an opportunity for empowerment. Anger often stems from a party's lack of understanding of the other's personal experience, resource constraints or cultural disposition. In such instances, the expression of anger may signal an opportunity for greater recognition of another's point of view. To ignore, sidestep or stifle expressions of emotion is thus to squander the opportunities for empowerment and recognition that these expressions present, and to negate the objectives of a transformative approach to practice.

It is surprising how many texts and training materials directly advise mediators to steer the parties away from emotional expressions and to control them tightly when they occur. The only value attached to emotional expression is the "venting" effect, i e , getting rid of the emotional "static" in order to deal more clearly with the "real issues". The transformative practitioner allows and encourages the parties to express their feelings, not to get rid of them, rechannel them or delve into their sources, but rather to uncover what lies behind them that might contribute to empowerment or recognition - as discussed in brief above. Therefore, when parties express emotions, the mediator does not just "wait until it's over" and then go on with issue discussion. Instead, she asks the parties both to describe their feelings and - perhaps more important - to describe *the situations and events that gave rise to them.* These descriptions of "the facts behind the feelings" very often reveal specific points that the parties are struggling to deal with, both to gain control over their situation, and to understand and be understood by the other party. When these points are revealed, the mediator can help the parties deal with them as they choose, directly and clearly.

Thus, instead of treating emotion as "static" to be vented and removed, the hallmark of transformative practice is that the mediator treats emotion as a rich form of expression which, when "unpacked" and understood, can reveal plentiful information about the parties' views of their situation and each other - information that can then be used to foster both empowerment and recognition.

6. "Clarity Emerges from Confusion": Allowing For and Exploring Parties' Uncertainty.

Intervenors who understand the transformative framework expect that disputants will frequently be unclear and uncertain about what the issues are, what they want from each other, or what would be "right" choices for them. Indeed, the intervenor sees that such unclarity presents important opportunities for empowerment. Therefore, another hallmark of transformative practice is allowing, and sometimes even encouraging, the parties to explore the sources of their confusion and uncertainty.

In practical terms, this means that the intervenor is willing to "follow the disputants around" as they talk through and discover for themselves what is at stake, how they see the situation, what they believe the other party is up to, and what they see as viable options. The mediator is comfortable with having the parties take considerable time to sort through what the conflict is about; and he can accept the lack of closure, if the disputants cannot settle on a clear sense of what the past has been about or what the future should be.

In thinking through what this means for practice, one experienced mediator made a somewhat paradoxical observation. She suggested that it is not always helpful to assume you understand a dispute too soon in an intervention. She said that, as she has gained experience in the third party role, she has come to believe that she is probably doing well during a mediation when "she is not sure what the dispute is about after an hour or so into a session." Rather than feeling a sense of panic about this ambiguity, she now feels comfortable with it and sees it, in some ways, as a sign of her ability to keep control in the parties' hands. Her comfort with ambiguity allows her to remain open, well into a session, to the parties' need to clarify for themselves what the issues are and what they want to do about them. It allows her to give the parties time to clarify for themselves what the conflict is about.

Recall the example given in the opening section of this article, of the party who keeps "wandering around" from issue to issue, point to point. A response to this situation along the lines suggested here would be one good indication that a mediator is carrying the transformative framework into practice.

7. "The Action is 'In the Room'": Remaining Focused on the Here and Now of the Conflict Interaction.

In the transformative approach to practice, third parties remain closely focused on the here and now, on the stream of individual comments and moves that parties make throughout the session. That is, the intervenor gives her attention to the discussion itself that is going on "in the room" - to each statement the disputants make, and to what is going on between them - rather than "backing up" to a broader view that focuses on the identification and solution of the problem that the parties are facing. The third party avoids looking at the unfolding conflict interaction through a problem/solution template, because doing so would make it hard to spot and capture opportunities for empowerment and recognition.

Instead, the mediator focuses on the specific statements the parties are making in the session (verbally or nonverbally) about how they want to be seen, what is important to them, why these issues matter, what choices they want to make, and so on. The mediator uses this close-up focus to spot precisely the points where parties are unclear, where choices are presented, where parties feel misunderstood, where they may have misunderstood the other - that is, points where the potential exists for empowerment or recognition. When she spots such points, the third party takes advantage of the microfocus to slow down the discussion and take time to work with the parties, together or separately, on clarification, decision making, communication and perspective-taking - i.e., the processes of empowerment and recognition.

This pattern of adopting a focus on the disputants' conflict interaction during the here and now of the intervention is a clear hallmark of transformative practice. It shows that the mediator is taking a responsive rather than a directive role in the intervention. And it shows that the mediator is concentrating on the goals of empowerment and recognition, allowing the problem definition and solutions to emerge from the parties' own perceptions and decisions. To put it differently, the transformative practitioner realizes that, while the *parties* work on defining and solving the problem "out there," the *intervenor* should be working on enriching the parties' working process - their decision making and perspective-taking - "in the room" itself.

8. "Discussing the Past Has Value to the Present": Being Responsive to Parties' Statements about Past Events.

When they are following a transformative approach to practice, third parties not only allow but even encourage disputants to talk about past events - the history of the conflict - because doing so is often a very good way to achieve the goals of empowerment and recognition.

Parties' comments about the past can be highly relevant to the present, in the unfolding conflict interaction. In talking about what happened, disputants reveal important points about how they see, and want to be seen by, the other party. That is, statements about "who did what to whom," rather than useless recyclings of history, reflect the parties' characterizations of both self and other in the present. In these statements, the parties are saying who they are, and who they think the other party is - today.

These kinds of statements lay crucial foundations for whatever recognition the parties may choose to give one another - for example, by reconsidering and revising their views of each other's motives, conduct, or character. Without the foundation laid by discussion of the past, exchanges of recognition in the present are unlikely if not impossible. The transformative practitioner pursues discussion of the past in order to build foundations for exchanges of recognition in the present; she then invites and helps parties - without in any way pressuring them - to reconsider their views of the past, if they wish, and to see if they want to extend recognition to the other party.

Similarly, when parties review the past, they frequently reveal to themselves (and each other) the choices they had at various points along the way. They become aware of key turning points, as well as resources and options they had available to them which went unnoticed. When this happens, disputants often take a new look at the resources, choices, abilities, they currently have available to them - a step towards empowerment.

Just as they advise against encouraging expression of emotions (see Point 5. above), many "how-to" manuals advise third parties to "focus on the future, not the past", and to encourage parties to limit their discussion of past events to a minimum. However, if third parties view the history of a conflict as a necessary evil - as something that the session quickly must move beyond - then important opportunities for empowerment and recognition will almost certainly be missed. An important hallmark of transformative practice is a willingness to "mine" the past for its value to the present - in particular, for the opportunities it offers parties to clarify their choices and reconsider their views of one another.

9. "Conflict Can Be a Long-Term Affair": Viewing an Intervention as One Point in a Larger Sequence of Conflict Interaction.

Intervenors who understand the transformative framework are aware that they are stepping into a stream of interaction that has begun before the intervention and, in most cases, will continue in some form after the intervention is finished. In practical terms, this means that the intervenor views the intervention as one point within a longer time frame. He does not view the intervention as resolving the entire conflict. This "long-term" view of conflict - and the attitude of acceptance and calmness about the limits and vicissitudes of intervention that flows from it - is another hallmark of transformative practice.

Thus, third parties following the transformative approach are more likely to believe that no single intervention will be able to address all the dimensions of a conflict in their entirety. They realize that, in many cases, not all the work the parties need to do can be done during the intervention. They recognize that even agreeing to terms of a settlement is not the same as carrying them out. Instead, their attitude is that it is a valuable accomplishment of an intervention (and a more realistic one), if the parties can establish a firmer footing, based on greater empowerment and recognition, that they can stand on as their interaction continues beyond the session. Sometimes this footing takes the form of concrete terms of settlement and sometimes it may not get that far. This outlook is crucial in enabling the intervenor to avoid taking a directive stance aimed at only one measure of success – settlement.

Seeing the intervention as one point in a stream of conflict interaction also gives third parties an awareness of the *cycles* that conflict interaction is likely to go through. Third parties following a transformative approach expect disputants to move toward and away from each other (and a possible agreement) as the conflict - and intervention - unfolds. This means that mediators do not fear failure when "progress" toward reaching an agreement stalls or deteriorates. They do not panic when parties come close to committing themselves to an agreement, and then back away quickly or unexpectedly, even near the "end" of an intervention. Rather, intervenors expect cycles of moving toward and away from agreements as parties wrestle with feelings of commitment and feelings of doubt and indecision. Transformative practitioners allow these cycles to happen and even welcome them, as further moments of deliberation and party empowerment. In short, they see such cycles as part of the natural cadence of intervention work.

Another good "test" of a mediator's operative commitment to transformative practice is the way he feels about and reacts to the kinds of limits and cycles typically encountered in conflict intervention.

10. "Small Steps Count": Feeling a Sense of Success when Empowerment and Recognition Occur, even in Small Degrees.

As any seasoned conflict intervenor knows, third party work is always challenging and often difficult. Feeling a sense of success is important in sustaining the energy and motivation necessary for practice. The hallmark of transformative practice lies in what it is that brings the intervenor that sense of success.

Transformative practitioners derive a sense of professional satisfaction when opportunities for empowerment and recognition are revealed during sessions, and when the parties are helped to respond to these opportunities -

if they choose to do so - in ways that advance personal strength and inter-personal understanding or compassion. Third parties committed to this approach are careful to mark for themselves (as well as the parties) the micro- as well as the macro-accomplishments of the session, and they do not define success solely in terms of the final agreement reached. Instead, they see and value the links between parties' micro accomplishments and their macro com-mitments. They realize that without discernible steps of empowerment and recognition, the value of any settlement may be illusory - since it is probably built on the shaky sands of third party directiveness. At the same time, they are convinced that, at the micro-level of empowerment and recognition, even small steps count; and they notice, and attach importance to, each step the parties have made along these two dimensions. Finally, when no agreement is reached, the intervenor realizes that actionable commitments can be made by the parties even after the intervention - and often are - if real steps toward empowerment and recognition have occurred during the process.

In short, what identifies the intervenor who is genuinely committed to transformative practice is what she says - and feels - when asked, after a case, "How did it go?" As with the first hallmark we discussed, it is the view of "success" that distinguishes the transformative approach to practice.

Uses of the Hallmarks of Practice: Strengthening Practice, Clarifying Theory and Expanding the Horizons

The hallmarks of practice described above are useful on a number of different levels. Indeed, several of the other articles in this special issue sug-gest how this is so, as they relate in varying degrees to the following points.

First, these hallmarks help to provide a more concrete guide for third party practice within a transformative framework. They provide a language and way of thinking about third party practice that is familiar and attractive to many intervenors, but often under-represented in the way practice is taught or evaluated. These articulated patterns of transformative approach can help form the basis for designing training, establishing new process ground rules and defining outcome measures that are rooted in a transformative view of conflict intervention.

For example, with the field now beginning to define "performance cri-teria" for assessing third party intervenors and trainees, hallmarks like the ones discussed here can help construct alternatives to more settlement-ori-ented assessment standards. Performance criteria can be defined on the basis suggested by these key indicators of transformative practice, allowing media-tors and students to evaluate themselves - and be evaluated - by standards that reflect the aims and values of a transformative framework, instead of adopting settlement production as the sole guiding value.

Practitioners and program administrators can also take a fresh look at the process ground rules around which intervention is structured, and assess whether these ground rules allow and support a form of practice that includes the hallmarks of the transformative approach. In addition, the hallmarks can help program administrators to design evaluation instruments that allow both disputants and intervenors to assess whether transformative objectives were met and how the third party assisted in reaching these objectives. In all these ways - many of which are already occurring - the hallmarks can support the work of translating the transformative framework into practice.

At the same time, the hallmarks of practice can also help, at a different level, to further a clear understanding of the framework itself - the transformative vision of conflict and conflict intervention. The details of the above discussion of these key patterns or habits of practice should help to dispel a common but serious misperception. Some take the view that the transformative theory of mediation, because of its emphasis on mediation's transformative effects, asks and encourages mediators or other intervenors to actively engage in efforts to "transform peoples' character". This misinterpretation confuses and conflates the transformative theory's claims about mediation's potential *effects* with the theory's suggestions about how the mediation process can and should be *conducted*.

The discussion here of the hallmarks of practice makes it clear that furthering party empowerment is one of the very cornerstones of this approach to practice. If third parties were to consciously try to "transform" disputants, or pursue any "agenda" beyond the parties' own wishes, this would directly negate the goal of empowerment. Attempting to change or transform the parties would be as directive as attempting to construct settlements for them. Clearly, this cannot be (and is not) what the transformative theory suggests for practice.

Describing the hallmarks of practice clarifies this distinction between the possible effects of mediation and the concrete goals and processes of a transformative approach to practice. As pointed out earlier in this article, if mediators follow an approach that concentrates on the specific *goals and processes of empowerment and recognition*, the experience of the mediation process itself offers the *possibility* of transformative *effects*. The focus of practice is on establishing and sustaining a context which allows parties to make clear and deliberate choices and to give consideration to other disputants' perspectives if they decide to do so. The third party is not there to *insist* on transformation, but to *assist* in identifying opportunities for empowerment and recognition, and to help the parties respond to those opportunities *as they wish*.

As clarified by the description of the hallmarks, the kinds of measures that transformative mediators take to foster empowerment and recognition are concrete - and limited - steps that are always dependent on and responsive to the parties' views and preferences. These steps ensure that *neither* party-defined solutions *nor* possible transformative effects are lost, as outcomes, as a result of a directive, settlement-oriented approach to practice. In sum, the point of transformative theory, as clarified by the discussion of the hallmarks of practice, is that when mediators focus on empowerment and recognition, *the mediation process itself* can give parties the chance not only to define and solve problems on their own terms, but to choose - without mediators' "moralizing" or other directive pressure - to act with autonomy and consideration for others and to strengthen their capacities for doing both.

Finally, the hallmarks of transformative practice provide clarification of another very important level. That is, they reveal that there are important connections between many diverse forms of third party work currently being conducted, and show that these diverse forms are all rooted in a similar, underlying transformative orientation to conflict and intervention. A review of these different forms of intervention reveals that the hallmarks described here are echoed in the general purpose and specific process characteristics of many current intervention efforts.

The patterns of practice discussed above are found in the work of intervenors using diverse processes in diverse conflict contexts - including environmental and public policy interventions, team-building efforts in organizational and corporate settings, and international/interethnic conflict handling processes. Thus, the identification and description of the hallmarks of transformative practice helps reveal the extent to which this form of practice is already being employed. As intervenors in many diverse contexts realize they are working out of a similar framework, they can more easily identify kindred spirits, and even establish a network that connects those committed to the transformative approach.

THREE

How Practical is Theory?

By Paul Charbonneau

Men live according to some gradually developing
and gradually withering vision. - D.H. Lawrence

Cris Trainer stayed up late one dark and dreary night, wondering about the mediation training program he was conducting with a colleague. "Why is it," he wondered, "some people just seem to get it, while others don't? Why are there mediators "out there" who, even after years of experience, still don't get it? Why the disconnect about what we are trying to impart in our training programs from what some people take away from the experience?"

Anyone who has trained or coached would-be mediators has at one time or another been baffled by people who just didn't seem "to get it." But what is the "it" we are talking about? I suspect the IT has to do with understanding, intuitively or by rational exploration, what mediation practice is *really* all about. It's about how someone envisions the mediator's role and the roles of the disputants. It's about the world seen from the mediator's chair, the world seen across the table and beyond. The IT is also about how the *trainer envisions* the world of mediation and what his or her understanding of mediation means for its teaching and practice.

If, as a trainer, I find myself wondering why some people don't get it, can I adequately articulate for myself as well as for others what IT is that they are supposed to get? As a trainer, what assumptions and premises do I hold that will tell me if someone has gotten it? Should these not be made explicit during a training? After all, they inescapably control the content and what is valued in a mediation training. They are the proverbial elephant in the room. They are the theory and power behind the training, whether they are explicitly acknowledged or not. Their importance cannot be exaggerated but perhaps has been too often ignored. As a consequence, training equips participants with a repertoire of strategies and techniques without a critical analysis of how and to what purpose the power of those skills is applied. **"Getting it' is about understanding by intuition or rational processes**

the theory or philosophy that defines mediation and shapes its practice.

This article explores not only the importance of theory in mediation training, but theory's requisite preeminence in understanding, imparting and practicing mediation from the transformative framework as articulated in *The Promise of Mediation* by Robert A. Baruch Bush and Joseph P. Folger (1994). The article also offers practical suggestions on how to integrate sound theory in mediation training programs.

Disturbers of the Peace

Training the trainer begins by challenging trainers to reexamine *for themselves* the theoretical foundations that shape their own thinking and goals when helping workshop participants "get it." Questioning one's own premises is always a risky enterprise. It can create doubt, shake foundations and lead to a more deeply secured and broad-based enterprise. In his *Letters to a Young Poet,* Rilke (1962), writes:

> And your doubt may become a good quality if you *train it.* It must become *knowing.* It must become critical. Ask it, whenever it wants to spoil something for you, *why* something is ugly, demand proofs from it, test it and you will find it perplexed and embarrassed perhaps, or perhaps rebellious. But don't give in, insist on arguments, act this way, watchful and consistent, every single time, and the day will arrive when from a destroyer it will become one of your best workers - perhaps the cleverest of all that are building at your life [author's italics].

Negative and sometimes hostile reactions to the transformative orientation illustrate Rilke's assertion that the doubt created by the challenges of a new approach to old assumptions can be experienced as a "destroyer." Experience, and my own in particular, teaches that the doubt engendered becomes one of our "best workers, perhaps, the cleverest of all" at building our practice. Doubt is among the best antidotes against sclerosis of the soul. It can transform a gradually withering vision into an expansive, invigorating vision.

Trainers need to think not only more deeply about mediation theory but also about its place in training programs, without fear of the challenges and confusion sparked by the discussion of the "theoretical."
Although many of us readily agree that good theory makes for good practice, we are loath to lecture about theory and want to avoid anything that smacks of the classroom or talking at people - formats spontaneously associated with teaching theory. In our effort to guarantee hands-on learning and experiential exercises to keep things moving and fast-paced, we have given

38

short shrift to theory building and have skimped on the materials that enable mediators to sharpen their vision and guide the application of their process skills. We may have inadvertently equipped would-be practitioners with only a menu of strategies and skills. Workshop participants often ask to have repeated some clever sounding, open-ended question, some reframed formulation so they can note it carefully, commit it to memory and later pull it from their plumber's toolbox to unblock resistance to a settlement. Instead, training must ask participants to reflect on the assumptions that accompany their enrollment in the program. **Training must make explicit what is implicitly assumed about mediation.**

Although an experienced mediator presents a significantly different profile than a novice, both, nonetheless, come to a basic or advanced training with a set of assumptions, either reinforced by years of practice or as part of the patrimony inherited by the average person-in-the-street. And that inheritance is generally replete with expectations about ways to get people to reach agreements, solve problems, and achieve win-win solutions. Would-be mediators, however, generally do not hold as fast to their assumptions about mediation as do experienced practitioners. Experienced mediators generally love their work. And they do not take easily to whatever might trouble their relationship with their practice and do not respond like sheep to one who would dare question the basis (premises) of that relationship and the practice orientation that has been the key to their "success" in the field. We are at the core of their professional identity.

Before going any further, it might be useful then to address a question frequently asked about training in the transformative approach: do the different visions and purposes of mediation practice actually need to be covered in an introductory training? Does a basic training need to compare and contrast the various orientations to mediation as an advanced training inevitably does? My own answer to this question is, "Yes," and for a number of reasons.

First, comparing and contrasting is a time-honored pedagogical method. I learn best about nutrition by comparing and contrasting the food groups. Second, a basic training is a kind of initiation rite into the mediation field. Beginners need some sense of what is going on in the profession and a clear appreciation of the fact that the field is not monolithic. There are fundamentally different practice orientations and new mediators ought not be allowed to infer from their training that there is only one orientation in the field and that the differences that may be "out there" are just a matter of style. Fourth, an introductory training that compares and contrasts approaches to mediation requires that the participants reflect on these differences. It enables them to surface their inherited assumptions and beliefs about the practice of mediation. As trainers explain their own conscious choice and commitment to the transformative approach, beginners must then, and perhaps as never before, internalize the premises and beliefs that drive the practice of transformative mediation. The choice to practice in this way will not result from not having been exposed to the values, premises and practices of other orientations. Their practice will be an educated, conscious choice.

"Getting it" is about vision and it's about mediation theory

The following questions, in one form or another, illustrate an essential introduction to mediation training:

- Is the practice of mediation visionary? And what is that vision?
- What are a mediator's viscerally held beliefs about conflict? the purpose of mediation? the roles, capabilities and rights of the parties?
- Is mediation value-free or value-driven? What is the alignment of beliefs, intentions and practice? How might misalignments manifest themselves?
- What about the varying and conflicting visions and purposes that shape the practice of mediation? What are the implications of directive, evaluative, problem-solving, transformative mediation?
- Are different approaches to mediation qualitatively the same? Are differences only matters of style? Or are they substantially different as a hammer is from a searchlight?
- Which orientation aligns best with an individual's own beliefs? For example, if I believe that mediation is about people staying in control of the decisions that affect them, then why might I control and drive their agenda and their process?
- And, dare it be asked, what rejuvenates the meaning of one's own practice? What makes the heart beat a little faster?

Finally, experience teaches that there is something about comparing and contrasting these orientations that creates resistance. However rich we grant that these questions are, we seem nonetheless reluctant to pose them at a training either because we lack the time or because we worry they will generate controversy. The old saw that comparisons are odious continues to influence us because, I suspect, comparisons invite controversy and maybe we do not yet accept emotionally that conflict is healthy. Because the field is growing apace, we can no longer shy away from our shared belief that conflict promises an opportunity for growth and understanding.

These hard questions promise to stretch and enhance our day-to-day practice for our clients and for ourselves. They are not the private, esoteric domain of scholars and theorists. They are the heart and soul of mediation practice and training.

There needs, then, to be a primary place for dialogue and argument in mediation training. **In our contemporary effort at openness to all points of view, we short-change our field and ourselves by avoiding an honest, rational testing of our beliefs about our goals and roles as mediators.**

As trainers we should see our role as that of disturbers of the peace, creators of doubt. We shut down differing viewpoints with conversation stoppers like, "Your opinion is important. Thank you for sharing it." End of discussion. In the name of openness, we unwittingly shut our minds and those of others to the sometimes painful but always enriching exploration of ideas and experiences. In so doing, we miss opportunities for opening our minds and deepening our understandings. In his book, *The Closing of the American Mind,* Harold Bloom (1987) writes: "Openness used to be the virtue that permitted us to seek the good by using reason. It now means accepting everything and denying reason's power".

As trainers and educators, when we are confronted with the inevitable "Yes, but" questions, we validate the questioner, but sidestep the question for fear that we might appear confrontational or defensive and "lose" our audience. We dread the possibility that a challenging, thought-provoking response to a questioner might "turn off" someone who will feel diminished by our disagreement with their observation and then accuse us of not practicing the recognition we preach.

When this happens we find ourselves closing our minds in the guise of being open to other viewpoints. A genuinely open mind welcomes an exchange of ideas, argument and a respectful request to clarify and support assertions and closely held beliefs. We close our minds and allow others to close theirs when we respond to queries with a simple, "That's true, too." Professor Deborah Tannen (1998) wisely reminds us: "Public discourse requires making an argument for a point of view, not having an argument - as in having a fight."

The entire conflict management field is diminished if we refuse or are unable to articulate and support the rational foundations and belief systems that inform our practice. We have become afraid of theory because it is open to questioning. And so we close it down, making mediation training safe and free from would-be conflicts.

We need to value controversy, not for itself, but as a training ground, as an opportunity to push further, to question and vigorously test assumptions and consequences, prejudices and resistances. This is not to say that workshops should become battlefields of ideas or exercises in contentiousness. The danger is that our training programs suppress differences and a thoughtful examination of those differences. We can model an appropriate dialogue. Tannen (1998) quotes the rules of engagement designed by Amitai Etzioni to make dialogue more constructive, "Engage in a dialogue of convictions. Don't be so reasonable and conciliatory that you lose touch with a core of beliefs you feel passionately about."

We would be best advised to profit from what our own life has taught us, that there is no learning without first unlearning, that there is no new vision without first experiencing the withering of some vision.

The best and worst arguments I have ever had have been with myself. And so it was with my own introduction to the transformative approach to mediation. Every question, every objection I have encountered in training new and experienced mediators in the transformative framework I have asked myself (and others) punishingly. Sparks sometimes flew. And they caught fire and awakened in me the enthusiasms and idealism of my youth. The experience recalls for me a radio interview with an aging symphony conductor who was asked how he got so much out of an orchestra. He answered simply, "I try to awaken in each member of the orchestra the fire they experienced the first time they played in a symphony."

Mediation training holds the potential of doing more than imparting skills: it's an opportunity to dream dreams and have visions about human beings in conflict, and the quality of their interaction. That can be the promise of theory. But it has to be talked about and talked about at some length. The time is past due to extend basic mediation training from forty-hours to sixty hours to accommodate this discussion.

Experiencing Theory

The challenge is to develop teaching methods that allow theory and vision to emerge from the participants' own experiences as re-lived through interactive training practices. These exercises become meaning-giving events. There are available to us interactive training methods that anchor the unabashedly lofty vision of transformative practice in the bedrock of sound theory.

For example, it is essential at the outset of a training program, to chart more than what each participant hopes to gain from the training. The trainers need to set the stage, proactively, and outline in as transparent a way as possible, *their* goals and methods as well as the mind-set that will shape their candid and respectful interaction with participants.

First off, trainers should make it known that they bring a bias to the training, that they intend to train mediators in a qualitatively distinct approach to mediation. To do this, they will ask, indeed push, participants to reexamine and question their own assumptions and beliefs about people, conflict and mediation. Ask participants to allow the trainers to be disturbers of the peace. They will say, "Yes." Have confidence in them. It's a hallmark of transformative practice (Folger and Bush, 1995).

With a soft touch, alert the participants that the workshop might trouble each person's fondly held relationship with his or her understanding of mediation. A trainer might tell the story of a most revered and sought-after Buddhist monk who, one day, placed outside his cave a sign that read, "Before you enter here to seek enlightenment, be prepared to abandon what you know." The monk died without ever having had another visitor.

Participants learn *first* that training is not just about skills-building; it's about giving meaning and direction to those skills. It's not only about what to do and how to say things, nor is it only about building a repertoire of clever formulations and open-ended questions; they learn that it's about knowing for what purpose mediator interventions are intended. Training provides experiences that prompt reflection. However Aristotelian it may sound, purpose defines. "What's a hammer, Mommy?", usually is answered with a description of what it does. Knowing how to swing a hammer without knowing its purpose is asking for trouble. **Well-grounded mediation training is about learning to understand and articulate the meaning and purpose of all those skills found in the much referenced mediator toolbox.** What is one attending to when the tool box is opened? Failing to ask, "What is the skill for, why this tactic?" assumes analogously and all too unclearly that it's like a hammer: made for banging. This is where theory must first come in.

In the language of the times, the theory piece is the foundation for "the vision thing." If we want people to get "It," we have to challenge ourselves with the question: As a trainer, can I convey clearly for myself and to others the "It" of transformative mediation? "*Ce qui se conçoit bien, s'énonce bien,*" according to the seventeenth century critic and poet, Boileau. Loosely translated, if you have truly got it, you can communicate it! And getting "It," is not only theoretical, it is experiential: it comes through a combination of processes: logic, deduction, induction, intuition, drawing, metaphor and, yes, reflection.

When would-be or experienced mediators register for a training in the transformative approach to mediation, they bring to it their own identities, professional experiences and assumptions about mediation. In large measure, they have already defined mediation for themselves. They bring a vision of themselves and their presumed role as mediator to the training. It's a kind of deep-seated, first-impressions-last kind of thing. They have a sense of the mediation trade; they now want to acquire or perfect its tricks.

When I ask novice mediators to write and compare their own definitions of mediation, the diversity of their definitions is enriching and insightful; on the other hand, this exercise exposes purely intuitive and frequently ill-defined notions. Definitions focus on reaching agreements and often run something like this: "Mediation is when two people reach a good compromise." And when asked to include a third party, they add, "with the help of a third party."

Ask workshop participants the question, "As would-be mediators or as experienced mediators, how would you describe your work to an eight-year-old child?" Answers range from "I help people reach agreements," to "I help people solve their problems." This exercise and those that follow bring to light the basic deep-seated and perhaps never-before questioned premise that mediation is about problem-solving and that a mediator's job, in plain unadorned language, is to get people to reach agreements.

Have participants list two spontaneous, uncensored word associations with "mediation." The result is a flip-chart sheet full of words like: problem-solving; compromise; concessions; giving in; solutions; agreements; ADR; better; neutral; confidential. No wonder clients are not knocking our doors down if those are the associations the average person makes about mediation. Words like process, communication, empowerment, recognition, change, dynamic, choice, discovery, perspectives, interaction seldom make the list.

An additional exercise that invites participants to revisit their assumptions about mediation follows a three-step process. The exercise was first suggested to me by Dorothy Della Noce and I further developed it in workshop settings. First, ask participants to work in small groups to answer the following broad question with its sub-questions: What have I heard about mediation? What's it about? What is the goal? What needs to happen? What do the parties want and need? What does the mediator do? What makes mediation successful? Next, chart their answers using their descriptors, then asking them to characterize their descriptions as evaluative or facilitative, process-oriented or goal-oriented, party-focused or mediator-focused? Thirdly, invite further reflection by asking: what belief systems or values are at work in these responses? As regards conflict? People in conflict? High and low expectations? Where and how is power and control exercised in the mediation process? And how do these beliefs drive mediator interventions? How do mediator moves align with one's beliefs about people, their motives, their abilities to solve their own problems and their right to self-determination? Only when these and similar questions get answered can mediators approach the table and pick up the tools of their trade with a clear sense of purpose. These answers become also the prism through which the coaching of role-plays takes on new dimensions, giving new vitality to the question, "Why did you do that?"

Lessons from Life

Revisiting premises not only about mediation, but about conflict, is a good place to start foundation building, too. One's understanding of mediation bears a family resemblance with its parent: conflict. **How I understand conflict will determine in large measure how I understand the mediation response to conflict.**

Conflict is frequently described in the literature as a perceived competition over values and/or resources; an incompatibility of needs and interests. Does our own experience of conflict square with these definitions? Is conflict about resources, values, substantive, quantifiable needs that appear unable to be met or honored?

At mediation training seminars and conflict management workshops, begin by exploring with participants their own experience of conflict. For example, ask participants to identify the first word they instinctively associate with conflict. Responses echo words like hurt, fight, war, pain, avoid, family. Words like challenge and resolution sometimes emerge. Then ask participants to choose quickly, avoiding self-censorship, what animal they would like to be in a conflict situation. Typical answers spawn a menagerie of lions, tigers, bears, eagles, scorpions and skunks. Few if any participants choose puppies, kittens, gerbils or lambs. The clear choice is what we could call a power animal. One thing we seem to have all learned from experience (in kindergarten, perhaps?) is that conflict situations suggest an urgent need for empowerment.

Invite participants to think of a conflict in which they have been personally involved and that they found particularly troublesome. Encourage them to draw how they saw themselves in that predicament. Most drawings will reveal small people, overpowered people, stick people confined in a hole, a box, a jar, trapped in a tunnel or flattened under a giant foot. One person depicted himself as a fire hydrant. Seldom will the drawings illustrate someone with access to information. The drawings will be about themselves in relationship to another person's behaviors. The experience of conflict is about the relational.

Divide the group into smaller groups; ask some to identify "what promotes effective conflict resolution" and the others "what prevents effective conflict resolution." Their answers are mirror images about *behaviors* that empower or disempower, acknowledge or diminish other people. Answers seldom have to do with the use of problem-solving skills, or other tools that can get problems resolved.

After a number of these or other similar brief exercises allowing participants to reflect on their own personal experience of conflict, everyone realizes that associations with conflict grow out of the impact that *dealing with* conflict has on one's own sense of self-worth and the failure to connect with others. The difficulty with conflict is not that it represents a tough problem to solve, but that interactions short-circuit the ability to connect and be understood. It's not the dispute; it's the disputing.

Conflict is not about insoluble problems; rather conflict is a crisis in human interaction; difficult dialogues need third party intervention when the process, the talking breaks down, when the quality of human interaction deteriorates.

How individuals relate to one another in conflict situations too often frustrates their need to go forward freely and confidently. Here begins the vision, based on experience, that mediation is less about problem-solving and more about the desire and need to change how humans interact. The focus of mediation becomes process. The mediator attends not to the problem but to the parties' process and their expressed desires to change their own dynamic.

Transformative Talk

When working with experienced mediators, it is an invaluable exercise to have them pair off and share with one another their personal mediation success stories. When mediators tell of their "favorite" or most meaningful mediations, they seldom talk about unravelling, by the expert application of their problem-solving skills, a mess of Gordian knots. Rather they tell about moments when the dynamic between individual disputants changed. More often than not, that change is about moments when individuals took charge and felt responsibility for themselves or reached out and extended recognition and a new appreciation of the other person's predicament. Mediators' success stories are spontaneously about transformation.

And here we are at the heart of the transformative approach to mediation: a mediation practice visioning conflict as a crisis in human interaction, intentional about responding to the parties' moment-to-moment, here-and-now calls for self-determination and connection with the other, in short, a practice focused on empowerment and recognition.

It is clear that mediation and the experience of conflict are about behaviors that in one incarnation or another have to do with empowerment and recognition; self-determination and personal autonomy; respect, acceptance and understanding. When those dynamics are fostered, the quality of interaction is enhanced and the parties engage in candid and frequently strategy-free conversations that produce for them the outcomes they need and desire.

It is only when this is understood that the mediator can take his or her place at the table, ready to respond to the parties' calls for empowerment and recognition, to be heard and understood, to have the freedom to choose confidently and wisely.

Unless mediation trainees are emotionally comfortable with this understanding of conflict and the mediation response, they will find themselves relying on their first and perhaps unexamined and unchallenged assumptions about people, conflict and their role as mediators, missing altogether the parties' aspirations for a change in their interaction. Saying, "Yes," emotionally to their understanding is the purpose of a solid and thoughtful approach to mediation theory.

Recognizing the conclusion that "[C]onflicts are constituted and sustained by the behaviors of the parties involved and their reactions to one another," has immediate consequences and implications for the mediator's mindset, for the application and practice of process skills, for training and for the development of mediation policies and procedures (Folger, Poole and Stutman, 1996).

Saying, "Yes," to conflict as a crisis in human interaction alters mediators' mindsets, and radically shifts their focus. Mediators re-orient themselves and the process, no longer towards a quantifiable, measurable outcome, but towards the dynamics of the process itself. Mediators are now positioned where the parties have invited them and one another to be: following and responding to each person's bids and offers for a change in their interaction, in their perception and understanding of one another's predicament. They inevitably address and most often repeat in the mediation room the behaviors and attitudes and concerns that have contributed to their communications process and that have not yet been appreciated or understood. The mediator encourages the parties to talk about what each believes is deserving of consideration by the other. That is what they have not succeeded in doing.

The mediator lets go of the instinct and inclination to respond selectively only to what the parties say that might be strategically helpful in reaching a concrete solution. The parties will focus on their interaction and may do it in such a way that may tempt the mediator to dismiss them as playing the blame game. **In reality, what appears as blaming may be an appeal for understanding or an acknowledgement of their sense of powerlessness.**

The practitioner learns to become deeply present to the unfolding "now" of the session, even, and perhaps especially, when the now calls up the past. If the past is relevant to the parties, it is relevant to the crisis in the interaction and is not judged by the mediator as irrelevant. The action is in the room, the past has meaning, and feelings about the past are what have brought the parties to seek the assistance of a conflict management specialist.

How the mediator intervenes flows directly from the orientation, the newly accepted mindset. Because the transformative approach responds to the parties' expressed need for empowerment and recognition, and because the parties' interaction during the mediation is most frequently driven by their own moment-to-moment responses to one another, **the mediator micro-focuses on the moments at hand, using established communication skills like summarizing, paraphrasing, reframing, to a new purpose: not to lead the parties in the mediator's preferred direction, but to invite elaboration and responses to their signals for empowerment and recognition.**

One of the more obvious implications for mediation training is the allocation of time to this new understanding of conflict theory as the beacon that guides mediator interventions. In terms of skill-building, the parties' interaction requires the development of competencies that focus on that interaction. Micro-focus skills are essential. They need to be practiced and emphasized in traditional training role plays and practiced in new exercises that highlight critical moments and mediator responses. Traditional role playing needs to be supplemented and matched by an equal allocation of time to micro-focus exercises. These exercises allow trainees to recognize and respond to key moments as they unfold in the mediation. When a party says, "This is a waste of time," a trainee learns that a skilled mediator's response at that instant is crucial. A wealth of understanding can be mined from that terse statement.

Micro-focus exercises feature "critical moments" wherein parties ask for or offer empowerment and recognition. For example: "That's not fair! What do you mean I haven't been doing my job?! I've been breaking my back trying to do what I'm supposed to and all I hear is that I'm messing up all the time!" That moment is crucial to the parties' interaction and is not a call for the mediator to change the subject of the conversation. Micro-focus exercises enable mediators to recognize the call and to devise an appropriate response and to gain greater clarity about the purpose of their interventions.

Thinking and acting from the realization that conflict is about interaction has implications for the definition of mediation and how that meaning can shape, restrict or expand policies and practice. Assumptions about what motivates people, what triggers conflict, how people *should* behave in conflict situations, what people are capable of and what it takes to resolve a conflict are questions that call for an immediate reexamination.

How does the certification of mediators change if conflict is not so much about joint problem-solving as it is about transforming the quality of the parties' interaction? What does that mean for legislators and policy-makers? How is mediator competence to be assessed? How is successful mediation to be defined and measured? What are the implications for the development of Standards of Practice and the meaning of party-self-determination? **Nothing is more practical than the theory and values that will shape and define the profession and practice of mediation.**

Conclusion

The theory behind the transformative approach to mediation challenges many of our established beliefs about mediation and the role of the mediator and what constitutes sound and skillful mediation practice.

In his groundbreaking book, *The Leader as Martial Artist,* Arnold Mindell (1993) comments on the "edges" that appear in workshops, the "forbidden communications" about "idealistic visions." He writes: "The best facilitators are assistants in human development; they are awakeners who gently encourage us to realize when we freeze in a role and lose access to the rest of our parts."

Because the transformative approach to mediation questions premises and assumptions about the practice of mediation which has spread in popularity and demand so rapidly in recent years, it is inevitable that cries of "you can't argue with success" will be heard. Mediation trainers must risk, gently and with respect always, starting a fire to thaw frozen roles and practices. **And there is no way that trainers can gently assist in human development without first attending to idealistic visions and the theories that nourish and sustain them.** Mindful of the quality of their interaction with participants, trainers will pursue a thorough, penetrating and true examination of what has become known as transformative practice.

They will, like Socrates, practice the midwifery of discovery, helping participants to give birth, sometimes painfully and laboriously, to that with which they are already pregnant: the universal hunger for empowerment and recognition.

FOUR

Myths and Misconceptions
about the Transformative Orientation

By Dorothy J. Della Noce, Robert A. Baruch Bush & Joseph P. Folger

A great deal has been said and written about the transformative approach to practice ever since *The Promise of Mediation* was published. The conversation that has unfolded about the framework has been useful in clarifying the underlying premises of the work as well as articulating what the approach looks like in practice. Although there has been significant clarification (and development) of the ideas over the past six years, several important misconceptions persist about the transformative framework and the form of practice that flows from it. These misconceptions often surface during training sessions when participants discuss their sense of what the transformative approach is and what can be expected from it.

In this chapter we briefly discuss seven frequently heard myths about the transformative orientation. We present each myth as we often hear it stated and then explain why each myth is based on a misconception about the theoretical framework or the way mediators practice within it.

Myth #1: Disputes do not get resolved.

Within the transformative framework, conflicts do indeed "get resolved" - but they get resolved by the parties rather than by the mediator. The mediator assists the parties by maintaining a focus on (1) the process by which the parties define and achieve resolution, and (2) a broad conception of what "resolution" can be.

The goals of a mediator in the transformative orientation are to foster empowerment and recognition. Thus, the mediator intervenes to support party deliberation and decision-making, and inter-party understanding, rather than to shape any particular settlement or to press for a settlement at all. However, by fostering empowerment and recognition when those opportunities arise in the parties' own conversation, the mediator assists the parties in clarifying and deciding *for themselves* what they consider a successful resolution. While the parties might decide, in their conversational decision-making process, that a successful resolution is an agreement, they might also define successful resolution as the decision to end the mediation without an agreement, to take the case to other forums, to drop the case, or to be satisfied with a better understanding of the events and circumstances that led to the conflict.

By focusing firmly on the parties' own moment-by-moment deliberation, decision-making and perspective-taking, the mediators encourage genuine, voluntary, fully informed settlements to emerge as and when the parties deem it appropriate. But they do not coerce agreements or define agreement in advance *for the parties* as the only possible successful outcome. Agreement is simply one decision the parties *may* make if they choose to do so.

Myth #2: It's only for cases where the parties "have a relationship."

Some people assume that transformative mediation is appropriate only in those cases where the parties have or want to continue a relationship. This interpretation misunderstands the framework.

Within this framework, every human interaction is a "relationship" - a process of interacting and relating - that can be conducted in a negative and destructive fashion or in a positive and constructive fashion. Therefore, in any situation where the quality of the interaction matters to the parties, and where the quality of the interaction will have an impact on other dimensions of the outcome (including whether agreement is reached and the quality of the agreement reached), interventions that help shift the interaction from negative to positive are of fundamental value. The interaction between an insurance adjuster and claimant is as vulnerable to destructive or productive influences as that of two neighbors or a divorcing couple. **Conflict is essentially about gaining clarity about decisions and choices (empowerment) in light of the experience of the other (recognition) in whatever setting it occurs.**

Myth #3: The mediators don't do anything.

Mediators from the transformative orientation are not directive. However, they are *proactive*. That is, they are actively engaged with the parties in conversation, listening intently for cues that offer opportunities to work with empowerment and recognition, highlighting those opportunities for the parties, and constantly inviting and encouraging the parties to engage in a constructive dialogue, to consider new information and alternative points of view, to gain clarity, to deliberate or "think out loud," and to make decisions for themselves. Mediators frequently "check in" to see where the parties would like to head next. They offer careful summaries of what parties have said, they ask whether anything that has been said by another party is "news," or, if they sense that one party is uncomfortable with the unfolding interaction, they may ask if the party may want to address what is bothering them. All of these various behaviors are active moves mediators make as they follow the parties through their path through empowerment and recognition.

Myth #4: All the mediators do is ask, "How do you feel about that?"

The mediator's primary task is to "follow the parties:" maintaining a micro-focus on their moment-to-moment conversation to identify and highlight opportunities for empowerment and recognition. So, at times, "How do you feel about that?" may be an entirely appropriate response to something a party has just said, if the question is used to invite clarification, foster reflection, or otherwise work with the opportunities for empowerment and recognition the party presented.

However, it is not the only, or even the primary, intervention of the mediator. There are times when it could be an inappropriate, intrusive or even directive response, particularly if the parties are not themselves talking at the level of feelings. It will depend upon what the parties just said, and what opportunity they presented. Probing for further clarification of feelings or attitudes is just one of many possible responses a mediator might make in working with the parties. **Mediators working within the transformative framework are skilled at reading the unfolding context, a context that is continuously created as the parties' interact.** Without such sensitivity to where the parties are, mediators cannot support where the parties want to head with their conflict.

Myth #5: There's no structure or order to the process.

The mediator does not impose a highly-structured process upon the parties when working from the transformative orientation. Imposing process structure has an (often unacknowledged) influence on the parties' conflict. However, this does not mean that the process lacks order and structure. **Order and structure emerge from the conversations of the mediator and the parties, from moment to moment.** The mediator does not have to impose a structure on the parties; parties are capable of structuring and ordering their conversations as they need to.

The mediator helps the parties determine how they want to structure their interaction by focusing on empowerment and recognition. For example, the mediator frames the goals of mediation in the opening conversation with the parties, and invites them to begin to participate in structuring the process by discussing whether they need ground rules and what those ground rules might be. The mediator flags "process decisions" for the parties, such as what topics they want to discuss, and whether they want to transition from one topic to another. As the parties make these decisions, the process naturally takes shape.

This more party-driven view of the process and structure of mediation enables parties to move in one direction for awhile, then backtrack and retrace their steps, reconsider where they see themselves heading and then move forward again in a slightly different (or the same) direction. This more cyclical view of the process is consistent with the way productive conflict interaction typically evolves and discourages mediator directiveness through process control.

Myth #6: A mediator can combine theoretical frameworks, or shift strategically between frameworks.

Mediators (and others) sometimes ask whether it is possible to combine the transformative and problem solving frameworks, to "do both" at the same time, or to shift strategically from one framework to another in the course of a mediation. Such combinations and/or strategic shifts are not possible for a number of reasons.

First, the two theoretical frameworks are based upon deeply-held beliefs about conflict and its resolution that are fundamentally incompatible. That is, one cannot hold both sets of beliefs and goals at the same time, or shift between them in a matter of moments.

In addition, the mediator practices that are characteristic of each theoretical framework are incompatible. For example, a mediator cannot simultaneously operate with a micro-focus on interaction and a macro-focus on outcome, nor can a mediator simultaneously support autonomous party decision-making and substitute the mediator's judgment for that of the parties.

One theoretical framework is inevitably favored over another by each mediator or mediation program, depending upon the goals and values of the mediator and the program in which the mediator works. Some mediators indicate that, during an unfolding session, they adopt a transformative focus on empowerment and recognition initially, but move from this approach when the parties get "stuck" or reach impasse. They then feel the need to change orientations and work from a problem-solving/settlement orientation. This role-switching approach ultimately leaves the actual mediation practice out of the realm of the transformative framework. It is like decision-making groups that say they run their meetings by consensus but switch to majority voting when consensus cannot be reached. Keeping open the notion of switching process commitments fundamentally changes the orientation of the group to its process. In the same sense, mediators who leave open the option of switching orientations fundamentally invalidate the goals of the transformative approach itself.

Myth #7: Transformative mediation imposes a set of values on the parties while an interest-based/problem solving model does not.

The Promise of Mediation clarified that all forms of mediation practice are based on world views – ways of thinking about what productive conflict is, what human beings are capable of and what third parties should do as they intervene. Transformative mediation is based on a set of relational values. Problem solving is based on a set of values that stem from interest based negotiation approaches to conflict. These values are clearly different. Because problem solving has been such a predominant view of conflict, it is often easy to think that this approach to practice is value-free, not built on any particular world view. This is clearly not the case. **To choose any approach to practice is to choose a set of values. We inevitably assume that the values we are choosing are the ones that mediation should be built upon.**

Conclusion

Trainers will often hear these myths in comments participants make during a training or see trainees practicing mediation based on these false conceptions about the framework. It is useful for any trainer to think through these issues carefully before beginning a training, so that clear responses can be provided when they arise. It is also useful to include summaries of these (and other) myths about transformative practice in training materials. Clarifying these common misunderstandings is helpful in allowing participants to understand the framework and to practice with clarity of purpose.

FIVE

Who Owns What in Mediation?:

Seeing the Link Between Process and Content

By Joseph P. Folger

Long before the term "sound bite" was coined to capture terse state-ments that media personalities strive to make, people have used memorable expressions to capture small truths. Many of these adages are intended as advice-giving, catchy quips people can rely on as they make decisions about how to act, what to say, or how to direct their lives. These frequently repeat-ed expressions run the gamut from the traditional, "You can't beat city hall," "Drink milk for health," "An apple a day keeps the doctor away," or "You can't go home again," to the more contemporary, "Bet with your head not over it," or, "It's better to burn out than rust shut."

The power of these adages is that they often carry nuggets of truth in them. But, like many simplified ideas, adages also hold hidden assumptions that can mislead or misguide if they are adopted without careful scrutiny or if they are applied in inappropriate contexts. "Betting with your head not over it," – a saying started by profitable casinos – may sound like good advice to those who gamble regularly, but the adage assumes that gambling itself is acceptable behavior. For many, any gambling – with or without one's head – is risk-taking behavior that is destructive and should be avoided. Drinking milk for health, although long seen as sensible eating advice, is now hotly debated, and not advocated by many dietitians and pediatricians. As market-ing tools or as simple advice, these adages should be accompanied with a "buyer beware" label.

A Widely Known Mediation Adage

Like any professional field, mediation has had its share of favored apho-risms. Some have been bumper sticker quips that are intended for public consumption like, "Mediate, don't litigate," or "Mediators do it until every-one's happy." Other sayings have been coined for internal consumption, as helpful sayings for practicing mediators within the field. One saying in particular has been a guiding adage for many practitioners, especially beginning mediators who often struggle with defining their third party role. **This adage, quoted often in training sessions and manuals, is, "Mediators own the process, parties own the content."** This rule has been a handy guideline for mediators; it provides a focus for mediators' behavior, shaping decisions mediators might make about what to do or not do in a session.

The most common interpretation of this maxim is that mediators should guide and accept responsibility for the mediation process, including setting ground rules, regulating parties' interaction, setting agendas, deciding when caucuses are needed, etc. Mediators have the responsibility for setting up and guiding a process that allows the parties to work constructively on their issues. The parties, on the other hand, need to control the substance of their dispute. They should articulate the issues, shape what gets discussed and, in the end, determine the mediated outcomes of their conflict. This "content" work is seen as separate from process considerations and is left to the parties, as a defining characteristic of mediation.

Like most adages, the content/process saying holds a kernel of truth that mediators have found particularly appealing. The phrase emphasizes the value of party self-determination and encourages mediators to place this value at the heart of the process. The saying makes clear that the parties "own" the dispute and its outcomes. It suggests a boundary that mediators should strive not to cross, a boundary that protects the parties' freedom to control the "content" issues of their conflict. This value of self-determination lies at the heart of why mediation has long been the centerpiece of the alternative dispute resolution movement. It is the characteristic that distinguishes mediation from the whole range of adjudicative processes. At the same time, the saying suggests that this boundary can be honored while still leaving a clear role for the mediator. The mediator has responsibility for guiding the process as the parties work on their issues. The saying suggests that the parties should not be given responsibility for process decisions about how the session or the conflict interaction unfolds – that is a job left for the mediator.

Like most adages that hold kernels of truth, this one also holds an unexamined assumption. The saying was adopted and widely used in the mediation field before its underlying premise was carefully considered. **The saying's advice rests on the assumption that the mediation process and the parties' content are unrelated, that they are easily separable in practice.** It assumes that when mediators influence the process, they do not have an appreciable influence on the content of the conflict, on the substantive issues and outcomes of the dispute. This assumption leads mediators to believe that the distinction between content and process is as distinct as the

56

difference between, for instance, a waiter setting a table for a meal and a chef preparing the food. How a table is set can influence the overall satisfaction with a dining experience but it has no direct influence on the taste or flavor of the food served. Those who have accepted this adage have implicitly believed that process control may influence parties' satisfaction with a mediation session but not have appreciable influence over the substance or outcomes of the dispute.

Separating content and process is, in practice, impossible. The distinction between content and process is not at all like the relationship between setting the table and preparing the food. It is more like the relationship between how food is prepared and the way it ultimately tastes. Choices about frying, baking, or microwaving have a direct impact on the texture and taste of the food. **Similarly, process and content are intertwined – the choices made about process have a direct and inevitable influence on the way a conflict unfolds.** It is through an understanding of how process influences content that the nature and purpose of process can be understood in a transformative approach to practice.

Process Shapes Content

The link between process and content can be seen clearly if we accept that, at base, conflict is interaction. **When parties are in a mediation session "the conflict" is the interaction that unfolds between the parties as the session develops. Any process rules that are established inevitably influence the interaction and, as a result, the conflict.** This important point was made by Sara Cobb (1991) in her discussion of the role that communication plays in mediation. Cobb points out that "the content of the dispute is constructed through discourse processes, and in turn, these processes are a function of the content of the dispute". She made explicit the way in which the parties' interaction gives shape to the content of the conflict.

One need not get far into a mediation session before the link between process and content becomes apparent. **The decisions a mediator might make about process at the beginning of a session have direct influence over how the conflict is likely to unfold at that moment and throughout the entire session.** Consider some specific examples.

When people enter a mediation room, there can often be questions raised about who should be allowed to be there and who can participate in the session. The mediator often feels responsible for these decisions as the parties enter the room. Mediators often view this as a process decision they must make. They often make a decision on this matter by clarifying who was directly involved in the dispute and who might be there simply to provide support or corroboration for what someone else might be saying. No matter what decision the mediator makes – to allow or not allow certain people to participate in the session – the conflict interaction during the session will unfold differently depending on the outcome of this decision. What the conflict becomes during the session is heavily influenced by who contributes to the interaction and influences its direction.

Similarly, process decisions that define ground rules for how the parties interact with each other are directly related to the emerging content of the conflict. A process decision about who talks first in a mediation session has been shown to have a significant impact on how substantive issues are defined (Rifkin, Millen and Cobb, 1991). The story the first person tells tends to become the defining frame for the conflict, it becomes the defining reality that the other party or parties have to penetrate through. **If a mediator makes a decision about who should talk first, he or she is making a process decision that will ultimately shape the substantive conflict throughout the session.**

The influence the first speaker has on defining the conflict might be increased if the mediator imposed an additional ground rule of "no interruptions" as each party told their initial stories. Allowing the parties to interrupt if they want to may actually support a shared articulation of a conflict, rather than imposing the first speaker's substantive definition on the unfolding interaction in a mediation session. The "no interruptions" ground rule may influence an unfolding conflict in other ways as well. For some people, not interrupting is an unnatural and uncomfortable way of interacting, one that might thwart their ability to engage with each other, think clearly about what they are saying or convey acknowledgment for something the other party has conveyed. Given this restraint on interrupting, the way the conflict unfolds – even what gets said – can be very different than if no such restriction was imposed. It can truly shape the content of the conflict. What is important to recognize is that decisions about who participates in a mediation, who talks first, whether interruptions are allowed, etc. are intertwined with the content of the conflict – they shape how the conflict unfolds during a mediation session.

Transformative Practice and the Purpose Behind Process

Decisions mediators make about how to create the process of mediation are based on the mediators' assumptions about the purpose of mediation in general. How process is handled is tied to the underlying goals mediators have for their work. The purpose a mediator carries into the mediation room shapes the way he or she thinks about how process concerns should be approached.

For a practitioner working within the transformative framework, decisions about process are linked to the goals of party empowerment and inter-party recognition wherever possible. As a result, most decisions about process are treated the same as decisions parties have to make about other issues or concerns. Parties are allowed to consider the choices they could make about the way they want their interaction to unfold. **The mediator is there to support party empowerment and inter-party recognition as the disputants make decisions about who should be present, whether interruptions should be allowed, when they should stop participating in the mediation, etc.**

The work the parties do in making these choices is deeply embedded in all other issues they may want or need to address during a mediation session. **The very nature of their interaction – what they are and are not comfortable with as they talk with each other – is often at the heart of disputing parties' challenges and obstacles.** Seen in this light, when a mediator does not allow the parties to work out the terms for their own engagement with each other, he or she undermines the core value of self-determination. In the transformative framework, mediators recognize that they are not acting neutrally when they set process rules for the parties. There is a clear and constant sense that conflict is interaction and interaction is influenced by the process rules and choices that are set, worked out or imposed. Allowing the parties to engage each other about the terms for their own communication – through the interplay of empowerment and recognition – is intimately tied to the way mediators view their work in a transformative approach to practice.

Conclusion

The saying, "Mediators own the process and the parties own the content," is built on a misleading distinction between content and process. This adage is misleading in two ways. First, it leads mediators to believe that it is possible to make process decisions for the parties that do not shape "substantive" issues and outcomes of the conflict. This belief produces forms of mediator directiveness that often go unseen or unacknowledged. Second, it leads mediators to believe that conflict is something apart from the parties' interaction itself. **The parties way of engaging each other – their way of "doing conflict" – is at the heart of why conflict is challenging and destructive.** If mediators control decisions about the way parties "do conflict" they preempt parties' self-determination in a fundamental sense. They do not allow the parties to work through their conflict by relying on empowerment and recognition. **Parties' ability to work through decisions about how they interact with each other is at the core of productive conflict work.** It allows parties to address their own crisis in human interaction.

S I X

Understanding Conflict and Human Capacity:
The Role of Premises in Mediation Training

By Sally Ganong Pope & Robert A. Baruch Bush

The field of mediation attracts practitioners from a wide spectrum of professional backgrounds. Every article about mediation in the popular or professional press draws many who self-select themselves as mediators and sign up for mediation training. What is it that motivates people to become mediators? For many, it goes beyond a desire to help people in conflict to resolve problems and to become a "negotiations manager"; the deep appeal arises from a desire to change the way conflict is experienced in personal, social and public life. Even more fundamentally, **the concept of mediation speaks to premises, often unarticulated, about conflict and the capacity of human beings to change, strengthen self and respond to each other through the experience of conflict; and it is this optimism, this world view, that draws practitioners to the field.**[1]

Not all would agree. The controversy about facilitative and evaluative mediation, for example, appears on the surface to be about how to mediate, but actually makes clear that mediators disagree about the purpose of mediation, not just the methods to achieve an agreed purpose.[2] Often presented as an argument about techniques, the actual, but not explicit, controversy is about our underlying beliefs and goals as mediators. As commentators survey the

---

Reprinted from Family and Conciliation Courts Review, Vol. 38 No. 1, ©January 2000 41-47
2000 Sage Publications

1 In the development of mediation training for the REDRESSTM Mediation Program of the United States Postal Service, the authors, working with Joe Folger and Dorothy Della Noce, developed an approach to mediation training from the "transformative orientation" that attempts to make clear the premises underlying the mediation training – premises about the goals of mediation itself and the role of the mediator. This article draws on that experience of developing a training incorporating premises and delivering it to trainers and mediators across the United States.

2 See Kimberlee K. Kovach & Lela P. Love, Mapping Mediation: The Risks of Riskin's Grid, 3 Harv. Neg. L. Rev. 71 (1998) and Leonard L. Riskin, Understanding Mediators' Orientations, Strategies, and Techniques: A Grid for the Perplexed, 1 Harv. Neg. L. Rev. 7 (1996).

mediation terrain and argue about what they see, they are often looking at the view from very different houses. Within individual houses, the foundational values and premises may be shared, but may not have been examined and made explicit. Examination of the foundations, the premises, is helpful to understanding the differences in the field, and when introduced into mediation training helps mediators understand their goals for intervening in conflict as well as how to do so. This article summarizes the foundations of the transformative perspective, considers the value of introducing premises into training and describes some ways in which that might be done.[3]

The Intuitive Value of Practice

Ask any group of experienced mediators to recall highlights from their practice when something happened that they experienced as significant and valuable, whether or not the parties reached an agreement. The accounts of such moments, the "success stories," quickly produce a long list. Mediators readily recall moments when a party: "really heard what the other was saying," "showed persistence and commitment," "understood how he had hurt the other," "cleared up misunderstanding," or "realized for the first time what she wanted to happen." In some cases, the moment may have made an agreement possible or it made agreement irrelevant. Of even more significance is the fact that the event was seen as important and valued by the parties and the mediator even in situations where no agreement was reached.

Research supports what mediators know and value from their own experience. **Parties reported high satisfaction in mediation when they were able to deal with the issues they felt were important, had the opportunity to present their views fully, had a sense of being heard and were helped to better understand each other.** Even when no settlement was reached and even when they "did worse" in mediation than they might have in court, they were satisfied as a result of a process that helped achieve those results (Bush, 1996).

These achievements, which mediators intuitively value, and parties report as most important, are often considered incidental to the work of mediation. They are considered "nice" if they happen on the way to working on the substantive matters, but not something a mediator can or should try to produce. There is inconsistency in this viewpoint. The view of the mediator as a settlement "technician" carrying a "tool box" to fix up a settlement for the parties, is inconsistent with the appeal of mediation, what we

---

3 The summary here is necessarily abbreviated. For a fuller explanation, see Bush and Folger, The Promise of Mediation (1994), and Transformative Mediation and Third-Party Intervention: Ten Hallmarks of a Transformative Approach to Practice, Mediation Quarterly (1996).

know are the most valuable results which may be attained, and beliefs about potential for growth in conflict.

The Premises

Conflict presents opportunity – mediators are taught this belief as a basic principle – often with the Chinese character for conflict that represents both danger and opportunity. But what is the danger and what is the opportunity? A mediator with a transformative orientation believes conflict is a crisis in human relationship and interaction, and it could be, and often is, a starting point for destructive interactions between the persons involved. However, it also presents an opportunity to change the interaction from destructive to constructive. **A constructive interaction begins when the person in conflict reacts in ways that strengthen self and increase responsiveness to the other in spite of the reaction of the other and the host of usual physical, intellectual and emotional responses to conflict that make this difficult.** Thus, the mediator believes that conflict presents the opportunities for growth in these two dimensions: self-determination and responsiveness to another.

In order to see the opportunities presented by conflict, the mediator must have a belief in the capacity of human beings for change. **Accepting and trusting that innate capacity for movement toward self-determination and responsiveness to other human beings, like a plant growing toward the sunlight, is an essential premise to doing the work.** This underlying trust in the capacity of human beings is essential if the mediator is to work toward the goals of mediation: supporting the parties' movement in both dimensions. The mediator will support full deliberation and informed decision-making by the parties about all issues in the mediation, substantive and procedural, including whether there is a settlement that will resolve the issues. Understanding of their own goals, the resources available, the possible choices - and then making decisions about them – all help parties in conflict move from weakness to strength, the shift we call empowerment. At the same time, the mediator supports communication and voluntary and mutual perspective–taking by the parties. The resulting changes in understanding of each other can help parties move from self-absorption to greater responsiveness to one another, the shift we call recognition.

True change cannot be forced, so the mediator will only support the parties' efforts and help open doors for them to consider whether they wish to enter. The mediator is not interested in persuading the parties to go in any particular direction, including one leading to agreement, unless that is what they decide to do. The mediator is interested in helping the parties to talk and explore what they want to do, individually and together, in a positive and constructive interaction. The experience of the process has the potential to increase capacity in the individual to make decisions and communicate more effectively in other settings. It also has the potential to shift the experience of conflict itself from destructive to constructive regardless of the outcome of the mediation.

Given the premise of the human potential for shifts in both dimensions – weakness to strength and self-absorption to responsiveness - mediators are relieved of the need to create the result in mediation. The result can be left to the efforts of the parties. We can trust that they want to resolve the conflict in the best way possible on the basis of self-determination and consideration for the other. Acceptance of this premise, and reliance on it, guide the choices mediators make in working with the parties. Mediators will be responsive to the parties in their interventions in the conflict in ways that will support party choices and the opportunity to take the other into account in the choices. Choices may extend to all aspects of the mediation process, such as setting ground rules, as well as the actual decision-making about the issues in conflict. Since parties are trusted to be able to handle the situation as well as to make decisions, there is no need for the mediator to direct the flow of the conversation, to cut off discussion of certain subjects, to "soften" the parties' words by reframing, to generate options, or to persuade the parties to select an option or to encourage them to reach settlement at all.

Unlike directive mediators who are oriented to solving concrete problems and use persuasion to influence the parties to reach an agreement which the mediator believes is right, fair and realistic, the mediator with a transformative orientation focuses on the interaction in the moment and the opportunities it offers to work in both dimensions, empowerment and recognition. It is at this level of actual mediator interventions that the differences in orientation and approach become glaringly apparent. Our society places much value on experts and professionals. Many mediators have been, and still are, professionals in other settings, and find it difficult to give up the expert, advice-giving role, and learn how to turn the decision-making over to the parties while at the same time being helpful and supportive. Without understanding of the premises and some resonance with them, mediators will not relinquish the directive methods learned in social and professional settings, as well as in other mediation trainings.

Introducing Premises into Training

Many trainees do resonate with the articulation of the premises of transformative framework, particularly when those premises are the basis for their attraction to mediation. For them the presentation of premises simply articulates something they already "know" explicitly or implicitly and the challenge for them will be to act consistently as a mediator in accordance with the values. For others who resonate less with these premises, the challenge will be to consider exactly what they do believe and whether they want to try to act on the basis of values they don't think they fully embrace.

In transformative training, the premises underlying the transformative orientation are presented and a number of exercises are used to enable the trainees to connect with and consider the value of empowerment and recognition. For experienced mediators, asking them to describe their recollections of significant and valuable moments in mediations, the "success stories" as described above, puts them in touch with what they value in mediation. In debriefing this discussion, the trainer points out how the descriptions of what was valuable track the two dimensions of growth, as this is invariably the case. When the mediators are also asked what in the mediation process helped bring about the significant results, the trainees then start to think and talk about the ways in which a mediator may support the parties in reaching these important results.

Connecting trainees to their own experiences in other ways also enhances their understanding of empowerment and recognition and their value. In order to allow trainees themselves to experience the value of empowerment, an exercise called "Getting Clear" provides the opportunity for trainees to talk to a partner about a situation in their own personal or professional lives in which they feel unsure, uncertain or unclear about what they should do. The listening partner is asked to help the speaker to gain greater clarity or insight for himself or herself without being directive. Even with just fifteen minutes of talking about the situation, at least a few of the speakers report gaining clarity, developing new ways of thinking about their situation, seeing new choices and new ideas to deal with it, and even resolving the matter for themselves. Since becoming clear about a conflict situation is one aspect of empowerment, the trainees directly and personally experience the value of empowerment with this exercise, either through their own experience or by hearing others talk about the experience in positive terms.

Presentation, exercises and stories are also used in training to help trainees connect to the second dimension of growth – that of responsiveness to the other, or recognition. This dimension is often more difficult to experience in the training setting than that provided by the experience of the "Getting Clear" exercise. Certainly some of the responses to the success stories illustrate recognition at work in actual cases. Use of "difficult person" and "shifts happen" exercises, also illustrate the value of recognition to trainees from their own experience. Talking about a difficult person in their

65

own life to a partner who is asked to try to help the speaker see the difficult person in a new light, often does just that, but runs the risk of many participants trying to help the speaker solve the problem. Small group discussion of past events in their own lives where they experienced or observed a real shift in their own thinking about another person often produces powerful stories about those experiences, and helps the trainees to understand the value of this dimension of conflict transformation.

Once the premises are understood and the common training experiences establish the premises and goals of mediation as empowerment and recognition, the trainers and trainees have a common language and rationale to apply to the further experiences of observing and practicing mediation in role plays. The opportunities for empowerment and recognition happen moment to moment in mediation and matter more than any "result". Therefore, emphasis is placed on understanding the flow of opportunities and looking at "critical points" for intervention. Vignettes of critical points are used to analyze and construct responses. Role plays of longer duration are generally interrupted frequently by the trainers in order to focus on the actual responses to opportunities as they arise and to avoid continuing demonstrations of a directive line of questions or responses. Again, the common language and understanding provided before the practice of mediation provides the framework for the discussion and feedback.

Teaching mediation from the transformative orientation to beginning mediators with significant time devoted to the nature of conflict and the potential for growth in conflict unleashes excitement about the opportunities inherent in mediation – and in conflict. The experience of working with both beginning and advanced mediators has made clear the difficulty for many trainees of letting go of the outcome orientation to trust the parties to make the best decisions for themselves. Even trainees quite committed to the values and promise of mediation find it hard to truly let go in the moment to moment development of a mediation. It is hard, when hearing about the real problems faced by the people in front of you, not to start problem-solving for them rather than simply assisting them as they go through their own problem-solving process. We have no models in our society for this sort of professional or helping person. We are accustomed to the "expert" advice-giver and problem-solver. Many mediators in training have been in that role in other professions, such as lawyer, therapist or teacher. Becoming a mediator for them may be even more difficult since they must avoid applying other expert professional skills in the mediation setting. But even for those without such expert training, our culture with its activist, "can-do" approach to problems creates the model of the helper as adviser and solver.

A person may leave mediation training saying "I want to protect and defend weaker parties" or "I want to be sure the parties find the right solution." Those trainees have understood the premises underlying the training and decided they do not want to take a transformative orientation to practice. **By making the premises explicit, we are assisting our trainees to better understand mediation and the role of the mediator and to examine their own views and values for consistency with what is being asked of them.** If some choose not to become mediators or choose to move into a different mediator "house" with others who also see the mediator as an arbiter of fairness and particular results consonant with societal or mediator values, then a service has been provided to the trainees and to the field of mediation. Being clear about the purpose of practice is important, whatever the choices mediators make about how they see their role.

Conclusion

For those who are inspired to continue within a transformative orientation to practice, a training course that has articulated premises assisted the trainees to understand their choice and will help them to deliberately and successfully adopt the supportive, non-directive approach required for mediation. Trainees leave training with a rationale, with understanding of their goals and premises, not just a "tool box" of techniques. However, we offer one word of caution for mediators who choose to experiment with the transformative orientation, although with some skepticism. They may be surprised. Some mediators have found themselves transformed by the experience. The responsiveness and changes in the parties convince the mediator to trust them and the premises of the transformative framework.

PART II

Transformative Mediation Training:
Tools for Instruction

SEVEN

Mediation as a Transformative Process:
Insights on Structure and Movement

By Dorothy J. Della Noce

We need to be able to trust that something as simple
as a clear core of values and vision,
kept in motion through continuing dialogue,
can lead to order.

\- M. J. Wheatley (1992)

Introduction

Over the course of teaching the transformative framework to experienced mediators for several years, I have encountered a common question: "Where's the process?" With this question, or some variation of it, experienced mediators ask for a sense of structure, order and predictability. More often than not, their point of reference is some form of *stage model*, that is, a prescribed, structured sequence of goal-directed activities that progress toward the ultimate goal of agreement. Mediators note that the transformative framework does not appear to rely on stage models, and for mediators who are accustomed to thinking of the mediation process as a series of structured stages, this feels something like being lost in the woods without a map.

In this chapter, I address this concern about the structure and order of the mediation process. I begin by reviewing the nature and purpose of models in general, and stage models for mediation in particular. I examine the assumptions underlying stage models regarding the structure and movement of the mediation process, and discuss why these essentially individualist assumptions are incompatible with the transformative framework. I then propose relationally-based ways of thinking about, and representing, structure and movement in this process.

71

The Value and Danger of Models

Models are used to describe and explain the patterns and structures of social interaction, and thus provide a sense of order and predictability for processes and interactions that might otherwise appear random, chaotic, and unpredictable. For mediators, who intervene in the often chaotic and unpredictable process of other people's conflict, this makes models particularly comforting and appealing. Models provide a sense of order, predictability and control for mediation training as well as practice. In training, models help trainers impart, and trainees develop, a basic conceptual framework for the mediation process. This provides a sense of overall coherence, that is, a comprehensive process "map" to which trainers can refer and into which trainees can incorporate each newly acquired concept and skill. Likewise, in practice, models enhance a mediator's understanding of the what, why and how of their mediation activities, the types of interventions that are appropriate, and the consequences of intervention (Della Noce, 1997).

Although there are various ways to model social interaction, stage models dominate the mediation practice literature. There are almost as many versions of the stage model as there are books on mediation, and each author appears to have his or her own idea of the stages of the process and the order in which they occur.[1] Nonetheless, the fundamental premise that there are discrete sequential stages to the process appears to be accepted without question.

Stage models, in fact, have become part of the unexamined, taken-for-granted, "common sense" of the field, permeating mediation policy almost as deeply as they do the practice literature. For example, as early as 1984, Folberg and Taylor recommended that the teaching of stages be a required part of mediation training, and the use of stage models has been institutionalized in the training standards of such organizations as the Academy of Family

---

1 The practice literature provides these examples. Folberg and Taylor (1984) and Taylor (1988) identify seven stages: introduction, fact-finding and isolation of issues, creation of options and alternatives, negotiation and decision-making, clarification and writing a plan, legal review and processing, and implementation, review and revision. Haynes (1994) describes nine stages of a generic mediation process: recognizing the problem, choosing the arena, selecting the mediator, gathering the data /fact-finding, defining the problem, developing options, redefining positions, bargaining, and drafting the agreement. Kovach (1994) identifies nine stages: preliminary arrangements, mediator's introduction, opening statements by parties, information gathering, issue identification, option generation, bargaining and negotiation, agreement, and closure. Irving & Benjamin (1995) describe family mediation in four phases: assessment, pre-mediation, negotiation and follow-up. Moore (1996) suggests twelve stages: establishing a relationship with the disputing parties, selecting a strategy to guide mediation, collecting and analyzing background information, designing a detailed plan for mediation, building trust and cooperation, beginning the mediation session, defining issues and setting an agenda, uncovering hidden interests of the disputing parties, generating options for settlement, assessing options for settlement, final bargaining, and achieving formal settlement.

Mediators, The Massachusetts Association of Mediation Programs and Practitioners, and the Supreme Court of Virginia. Some approaches to mediator evaluation, such as those used by the Maryland Council for Dispute Resolution and The Massachusetts Association of Mediation Programs and Practitioners, contain the assumption that managing stage-specific tasks and a progression through stages is a required competency of a mediator. Virginia's Standards of Ethics and Professional Responsibility for Certified Mediators require that certified mediators describe "the stages" of the mediation process to the parties. And, in "Mediation: A Consumer Guide," published by the Virginia Department of Dispute Resolution Services, mediation is described as a process consisting of five stages.

But the taken for-granted knowledge and beliefs of any community, what is accepted as its "common sense," is not neutral and value-free. Rather, it is typically founded on deeply-held ideological premises and beliefs (van Dijk, 1998). Likewise, mediation stage models are not neutral, value-free representations of the social world. Rather, they reflect ideologically-based assumptions about how the social world operates, how people interact, what ends are desirable, and how those ends are best achieved. Models also perpetuate those ideologically-based assumptions: when practitioners use models prescriptively, they shape the social world to conform with the model. That is, as practitioners structure social interactions to conform with the model, they likewise foster those social interactions that are consistent with the assumptions upon which those models are built, and constrain the possibility of interactions based on different assumptions.

Thus, it is important to consider models critically: to surface, examine, and evaluate the assumptions on which they are based and the forms of social interaction they sustain (Fairclough 1989, 1995). In the next section, I discuss the assumptions about the structure and dynamics of mediation that underlie stage models for mediation practice, and how those assumptions emerge from and reproduce a particular view of the social world.

Linear Stage Models: Form Determines Function

Traditional stage models, no matter how they differ in the number of stages presented or the names of those stages, share certain fundamental premises about the *structure* of the mediation process and *movement* within it. These premises, in turn, reveal and sustain the individualist worldview.

Structure

The structure of stage models is typically linear, that is, they have a definite direction and an ideal end-state (Van Lear, 1996). Stages are organized to show sequential progress toward the desired goal, and each stage is viewed as the necessary prerequisite to the next. The very structure of stage models suggests that only forward movement toward the ideal end-state is desirable and normal. Although some authors describe stages as reflexive, or looping back, these descriptions usually imply that this is necessary when something about the process or the parties is not working as it should (see, e.g., Folberg and Taylor, 1984; Folberg and Milne, 1988; Irving and Benjamin, 1995; Kovach, 1994; Moore, 1996). Returning to any prior stage in the sequence is a way to take care of the unfinished business of that stage, so that progress forward may resume. Likewise, entering any stage prematurely is portrayed as detrimental to the process. For example, Haynes (1994) describes premature goal articulation, premature bargaining, and premature closure as process dangers the mediator must avoid.

For stage models of mediation, the goal of this linear progression, and the ultimate desired end-state, is agreement. This goal is practically compelled when mediation incorporates interest-based bargaining as an essential step or phase, which requires the mediator to encourage the parties to use interest-based bargaining, and then assist them in doing so, for the purpose of reaching an integrative, or win-win, agreement (see, e.g., Haynes, 1994; Irving and Benjamin, 1995; Menkel-Meadow, 1995; Mnookin, Peppet and Tulumello, 1996; Moore, 1996; Rubin, Pruitt and Kim, 1994; Slaikeu, 1996). Stage models encompass no other definition of success: a good mediation is one in which a win-win agreement is reached. Other outcomes can be explained only as a failure in the staged progression. With agreement as the only successful end result, stage models distort the goal of agreement from one that the parties may have to one that they *must* have. Agreement becomes an end-point which belongs to the *mediator's* overall plan, and which is presumed for the parties by the very structure of the process.

From Structure to Movement

In stage models, the emphasis is on the structure itself. These models seldom, if ever, explicitly describe how and why movement from one stage to another occurs. However, the source of movement is implied in the structure. **Progression through a series of sequential stages requires that someone manage or direct that progress. That someone must be the mediator: the mediator alone has the map.** He or she alone knows what the stages are and the order in which they should occur. Decisions about how and when to move from one stage to another typically belong to the mediator (see, e.g., Moore, 1996).

The structure of stage models practically compels mediators to lead the parties and direct their progression through the stages to the goal of agreement. Form determines function. The mediator succeeds in getting people to the goal of agreement by maintaining a focus on outcomes, structures, and strategies, or what Bush & Folger (1994) call a *"macro-focus."* A macro-focus encourages the mediator to get "ahead of the parties" (Kolb, 1994, p. 472). This, in turn, objectifies the parties, who are discussed as being *moved through* the process by the mediator but as having no significant influence on that movement (see, e.g., Haynes, 1994; Slaikeu, 1996).

Linear Models and Ideology

The premises of linearity and mediator control which inform stage models are part of a larger, ideologically-based approach to the world. Stage models are based on individualist assumptions about human interaction. This is seen most clearly in the way these models assume a *presocial* human being, that is, an atomistic and autonomous human being who exists separate and apart from social processes (Fairclough, 1989; cf. Della Noce, 1999). Only presocial human beings can be moved through a social process by another, yet remain essentially untouched and unchanged. The mediator, too, is portrayed as a presocial human being, able to move people through a social process yet remain separate from their world and their decisions, via theoretical constructs like mediator neutrality (cf. Cobb, 1991). Thus, the individualist mediator is "an isolated individual who is guided only by the organization of his or her mental processes" (Burkitt, 1999, p. 72; cf. Cobb and Rifkin, 1991; Della Noce, 1999).

Individualism also appears in the assumptions stage models make about the nature of the social world. Individualism assumes an objective social world "out there." Assumptions that the social world can be understood by reducing it to separate and discrete parts, to linear cause and effect, and to process maps that focus upon structure, in order to make it possible to strategically manipulate it toward preferred outcomes, proceed from a distinctly individualist worldview (Wheatley, 1992).

In summary, while stage models create a certain appearance of order and coherence, that order comes at a price. Linear sequential order demands mediator control, and encourages a mediator to exert his or her control over the process and the parties in particular ways. The parties become objects to be moved, and the mediator becomes, as Antes and others have observed, "a stage coach" (1999, p. 296). The mediator relates to the parties, and hence the parties relate to each other, in objectifying, instrumental ways, sustaining an individualist view of the world (Della Noce, 1999).

In the next section, I explore why and how relational assumptions suggest different ways of thinking about the structure and dynamics of the mediation process, and hence, different models.

Toward Relational Models of Social Interaction

The transformative framework represents a paradigm shift from the individualist worldview to a relational worldview (Bush and Folger, 1994), which has consequences for the construction of models. Because these paradigms are essentially incompatible, models built on the assumptions of one paradigm cannot simply be imported to another (Della Noce, 1999; cf. Hekman, 1995).

Relational ideology portrays the human world as socially and discursively constructed (Bush and Folger, 1994; Hekman, 1995; McNamee and Gergen, 1999). Human beings are depicted as fundamentally social, that is, formed in and through their relations with other human beings, essentially connected to others, and constantly relating to others through dialogue (Bush and Folger, 1994; Della Noce, 1999; Hekman, 1995; McNamee and Gergen, 1999). There are no firm boundaries between the self and the social (Della Noce, 1999). Social structures do not exist separately from the interactions that create and sustain them. Rather, social structures emerge from the interactions between people, particularly their unfolding, on-line, conversational interactions.

In the relational world, social phenomena are complex and non-linear; they cannot be reduced to separate and discrete parts, or simple maps of cause and effect (Wheatley, 1992). Seemingly separate parts are bound by relationships and interconnections. This is not a world on which one individual can or should impose order. A single actor does not produce order; rather, **order emerges from the ongoing interactions of all participants in the social situation.** Order must be understood as separate from "control" (Wheatley, 1992). To understand, describe and explain this world, we must think in terms of creative processes and dynamic, continuous change.

This relational view of the world is visible in the premises of the transformative framework for mediation. Mediation, when practiced as a transformative process, requires a *micro-focus*, rather than a macro-focus (Bush and Folger, 1994). The mediator's focus is on the dynamics of the moment-to-moment interaction between the parties rather than a single goal at the end of a series of stages (cf. Folger and Jones, 1994; Jones, 1994). The mediator attends to that conversational interaction for opportunities for deliberation and decision-making (empowerment), as well as opportunities for interpersonal understanding (recognition), and highlights these opportunities for the parties as they emerge. The parties then decide whether and how to respond to the opportunities.

With this paradigm shift from the linear, static individualist world to the dynamic relational world, **conflict becomes understood as created, constituted, and transformed in the mediation process through the ongoing communicative interaction of the parties and the mediator.** The understandings and interactions of people in conflict are assumed to move, change and grow throughout the mediation process. The focus of the mediator is on the potential for movement evident in the parties' discourse - from relative weakness, confusion, disorganization and uncertainty to greater clarity, confidence and strength (empowerment) and from relative self-absorption to greater openness and consideration for the situation and perspective of the other (recognition) - rather than an abstract structure in a mental model.

From the transformative framework, neither the mediators nor the parties stand apart from the social process of the evolving conflict or its resolution. Conflict and its resolution are discursively constituted in the course of the mediation. Because the parties are not objects to be moved through a series of stages, but are co-creators of an ongoing interaction, the parties' contributions to the conversation are closely monitored by the mediator as a source of clues to opportunities for empowerment and recognition. Thus, the mediator adopts a particular conversational stance with the parties: that of *following*, using a micro-focus, rather than leading or directing with a macro-focus (Bush and Folger, 1994; Folger and Bush, 1996; Grillo 1996; Pope 1996).

One consequence of this micro-focus on possibilities for change and growth through discourse is the elimination of agreement as the single, presumed and privileged end-state in the mediator's "map" of mediation. As the mediator highlights opportunities for empowerment and recognition, the parties' desired end-state emerges and evolves through their interaction. Agreements are but one possible outcome, which the mediator can and does help the parties reach, if they so choose, by fostering the parties' deliberation, decision-making, and interpersonal perspective-taking. At the same time, other outcomes are also possible, and may be valued by the parties as much or more than they value an agreement: for example, new insights on the dispute, greater clarity about choices and options, and new understandings of each other's views and situations (Bush and Folger, 1994; Folger and Bush, 1996). The ultimate end-state is the parties' choice.

The focus of the transformative framework on discourse and social interaction in a dynamic moment-by-moment social process explains why traditional stage models are inadequate, and indeed, counter-productive (cf.

Bush and Folger, 1994). The transformative framework does not reside within the individualist world (Bush and Folger, 1994). The question is how the relationally-based micro-focus on discursively-constituted movement, change and growth, and the absence of a single, presumed end-state, can translate into a model structure.

From Dynamics to Structure

What I will outline here is the current status of one evolving attempt to develop new concepts for modeling relational social processes. This effort began with a small group discussion among some colleagues in 1996, as part of the Training Design Consultation Project, and continues to this very day. I first presented the ideas on which this chapter is based, and a tentative model design, in May 1997 at the National Conference on Peacemaking and Conflict Resolution, and in July 1997 at the Annual Conference of the Academy of Family Mediators. Workshop participants in both of those conferences were generous with their insights and commentary. I have also continued to refine and expand these ideas through ongoing dialogue with a number of colleagues.[2] Bush, Folger, Della Noce and Pope published a modified version of the original model design in *Advanced Mediation Skills for Postal Service Mediators: Practice within a Transformative Framework* (1998). Meanwhile, Antes, et al., (1999) were simultaneously pursuing their own insights and model design.

I trace these efforts to give a sense of the exploratory nature of creating new models, and to situate my efforts as such. I do not propose to set forth "the" model for transformative mediation, so much as stimulate additional thinking on what models of relational social processes might look like. I invite others to join these efforts.

For those interested in pursuing the development of such models, I highly recommend two sources of additional reading. Wheatley (1992) provides a rich source of images and metaphors for relationally-based, dynamic processes. The work of communication scholars is also instructive. In contemporary communication science, stage models are criticized because they oversimplify complex behavior, focus on structures rather than dynamic interactions within social systems, and thereby limit thinking (see, e.g., Poole and Baldwin, 1996; Van Lear, 1996). They have been largely abandoned in favor of "evolutionary models" (Van Lear, 1996). Evolutionary models are

2 I would like to express my gratitude, in particular, to Joe Folger, Robert A. Baruch Bush, Bob Stains, Jim Antes, Donna Turner Hudson, Sally Pope, Phyllis Bernard, Paul Charbonneau and Judy Saul, for their insights, critiques, and continuing enthusiasm for constructive and creative dialogue. I would also like to credit Michael Della Noce for the assistance he provided in developing a graphic design.

those in which a single specific end-state is not the sole focus. Even in those cases where an end-state is specified, the focus is more on how various paths to the end-state are socially constructed. **Evolutionary models take into account that there are many turning points along the way and a variety of factors that interact to produce any one evolutionary course** (Van Lear, 1996). Whereas linear sequential models tend to be programmed by rules, plans and scripts, evolutionary models reflect creative, on-the-spot adaptations within a system of communication (Van Lear, 1996). Evolutionary models enable new forms of understanding, making possible the integration within a single model of both the micro-level dynamics of interaction and the macro-level sequences of activity which are structured by that interaction (Poole and Baldwin, 1996; Poole, Seibold and McPhee, 1996).

I also must point out that the model discussed here is conceptual and illustrative, designed to help mediation trainers and mediators understand a complex social process. This model is not based on empirical research, and such research is encouraged as a way of further exploring these ideas.

Modeling Order without Control: Form Follows Function

In my view, and consistent with the requirements of evolutionary models, a model of the transformative framework for mediation practice must capture: (1) the micro-level dynamics of movement through the process; (2) the interactively-constructed patterns of discourse which characterize mediation; and (3) the centrality of the principles of empowerment and recognition. A proposed model is depicted in Figure 1.

This model meets my first and third criteria by depicting empowerment and recognition as the theoretical driving forces of movement in the process. The dynamic interplay of empowerment and recognition, the dialogic tension between strength of self and concern for other - or autonomy and connection - stimulate movement in the mediation process (cf. Jones 1994). As the mediator focuses on highlighting empowerment and recognition opportunities that arise moment-by-moment in the parties' conversations, the nature of the parties' interactions develop, move, and shift through various spheres of activity. In depicting the interactive construction of these spheres of activity, the model meets my second criteria. As I will discuss in more detail below, by capturing micro-level dynamics and the patterns of activity shaped by these dynamics, the model provides a sense of the order and structure of the mediation process.

While I use the term "structure" to discuss the patterns of activity that emerge through this interaction, I do not use it to refer to static frameworks. Burkitt (1999) offers a useful term, describing structures that emerge in a con-

Figure 1: A model for medation as a transformative process

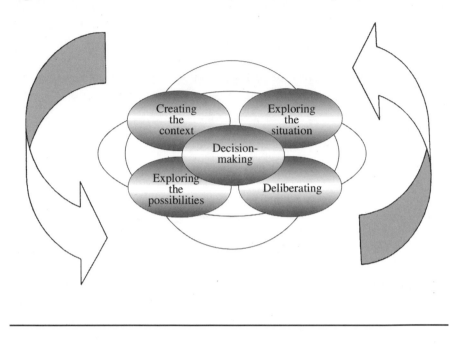

Outer Ring:
Mediator's focus
Attending to empowerment and recognition

Inner Ring:
Spheres of activity naturally shaped and reshaped
through the conversational interactions in the session

tinual process of reconstruction and reformulation through social practice as *generative structures*, for which he suggests metaphors of movement, music and dance. In the next section I discuss the emergent, generative structures made possible in this framework (cf. Antes et al., 1999).

Structure as Paths through Spheres of Activity

This model also reflects the premise that **structure and order need not be imposed, but will emerge from the interaction of the parties and the mediator, as the mediator attends to empowerment and recognition** (cf. Antes et al., 1999). This requires a certain amount of trust that social processes can take shape on their own, without a need to force them into any particular shape, which is contrary to the popular assumption that if mediation is to have a "form" the mediator must impose it. The group decision-making literature is instructive in this regard. Olaniran (1996), for example, distilled certain core activities that appear to be common to all joint decision-making processes (identifying the task or the difficulty, generating ideas and possible solutions, discussing implications, and reaching decisions), but noted that while these core activities are present to some extent in all joint decision-making interactions, no particular order prevails. As its members interact, each group develops its own unique decision-path (Olaniran, 1996).

Building on Olaniran's conceptualization, I propose that parties typically shape and move through five core spheres of activity in mediation, if the mediator attends to the opportunities for empowerment and recognition that emerge in their conversation. These essential spheres of activity are depicted in the center of Figure 1: *creating the context, exploring the situation, deliberating, exploring possibilities, and making decisions.* In the following paragraphs, I elaborate the activities that characterize each sphere.

Creating the context involves the creation of a social context for the parties' interactions and a shared understanding of the process. This encompasses discussions about whether to participate in the mediation, the roles of the mediator and the parties, how the process is expected to unfold, who should participate, possible outcomes, ground rules, time frames, confidentiality, and the use of caucus. It includes the opening conversation among the parties and the mediator, as well as opportunities to clarify and restructure the process throughout the mediation. Functionally, this sphere of activity involves the question, "How do we want to do this?"

Exploring the situation occurs when the parties discuss what brings them to the mediation, their situations and understandings, and what the experience of this conflict has been like for each of them. It involves discussions of the past as well as the present (Folger and Bush, 1996). Functionally, this sphere encompasses the question, "What is this about?" (cf. Antes et al., 1999).

Deliberating occurs when parties "observe and reflect on their own behavior and construct alternate views of the conflict situation" (Putnam 1994). "Deliberation" is a central concept among scholars exploring conflict transformation because it embraces the possibility of change in the conflict interaction (see, e.g., Bush and Folger 1994; Kolb and Putnam, 1997; Putnam 1994). Deliberation is a communal act (Mansbridge, 1990) as well as a reflective one. In the process of dialogue, deliberating parties observe their own thinking and step into the thinking of others (Kolb and Putnam, 1997), opening the possibility for greater clarity, new interpretations, new understandings and the development of shared meaning (Della Noce, 1999). Functionally, deliberation encompasses the question, "What does this mean?"

Exploring possibilities occurs whenever parties imagine, suggest, reject, or consider the implications of possibilities for dealing with the conflict. These possibilities include, for example, changing opinions or attributions, making apologies, changing behavior, making agreements, gathering information, mobilizing resources, seeking the assistance of another professional, continuing the conflict, escalating the conflict, or choosing another process. Functionally, this sphere encompasses the question, "What is possible?"

Decision-making occurs each time a party makes a choice. It appears at the center of the graphic, because the **parties are making decisions constantly throughout the process: about whether and how to interact, whether and how to extend recognition to the other, how to conduct the process, and about the substance and outcome of the dispute itself.** In this model, agreement can be considered one possibility within the decision-making sphere. It remains a part of the mediation model, as one of the many decisions open to the parties that may emerge and evolve during their social interaction, but it is no longer the single, privileged, and presumed endpoint of a linear process orchestrated by the mediator. Functionally, decision-making encompasses the question, "What do I/we do?" (cf. Antes, et al., 1999).

This model helps mediators understand, and trainers explain, certain key concepts in the transformative framework, which I describe in the next section.

Using the Model

The model places a *micro-focus on discourse,* illustrating how the mediator and the parties together shape the process through their conversational interaction. By placing the mediator's work in the outer ring, focused on the theory and dynamics of empowerment and recognition, the model demonstrates that the mediator's attention to empowerment and recognition opportunities at the micro-level permits the conversational interaction to develop naturally into the five spheres of intermediate activities.

The model also makes visible the *fluidity* of the process, showing that parties may enter and leave the process at any point, not simply at a designated linear entry and exit point, as well as the likelihood that the parties may naturally move from any one sphere of activity to any other, in any order. It also reflects the reality that multiple spheres may be in motion at the same time, as for example, when one party's comments during one turn at talk indicate that she is considering new information just offered by another party, that she is deciding it has merit and changes her perspective on the situation, and that it gives her new ideas to offer. Likewise, at any given moment each party may be in a different sphere. The key to moving through this system is to *follow the parties* through it, and to start and end where the parties are. There is no "wrong direction." Each mediation interaction will create its own unique decision-path.

Structure emerges as the parties move in and out of various spheres of activity, along the path and in the various directions that the parties themselves shape. The mediator does not have to move the parties from one sphere of activity to another. The mediator is thus freed from concerns with an abstract stage structure, and from concentrating on (let alone remembering) a fixed linear sequence of stages. The mediator need only focus on the principles of empowerment and recognition and how they emerge in the parties' micro-level dialogue.

The model also makes clear that training has two paramount goals: (1) developing understanding of the ideological and theoretical underpinnings of the transformative approach, and (2) building trainee comfort and facility in recognizing, working with, and responding to, opportunities for empowerment and recognition as they emerge in conversational interaction.

Conclusion

It is my hope that this chapter stimulates trainers and others to evaluate critically the taken-for-granted standard fare of mediation trainings, as well as the structures introduced into trainings and the assumptions on which they are based, and to consider adopting or developing new models for training based upon relational assumptions and the concepts of empowerment and recognition.

I also hope that this chapter spurs examination of the assumptions upon which training standards for mediation have been constructed, and how those assumptions shape what new mediators learn about the practice of mediation. As I noted in the beginning of this chapter, some organizations have institutionalized in their training standards the idea that mediation is a process composed of sequential stages. This chapter illustrates that institutionalizing something as seemingly innocuous as a stage model has social consequences: promoting an individualist view of the world and approach to mediation practice. It is not clear whether these consequences are the product of fully-informed, conscious choice or unreflected "common sense." But, I suggest that policy decisions about training content should be made in light of the growing body of research and theory in the field, in a reflective and critical process (Della Noce, 1999).

EIGHT

Beginning the Mediation:
Party Participation Promotes Empowerment
and Recognition

By Sally Ganong Pope

The mediation begins. The parties arrive. The mediator introduces herself and invites the parties to sit at the mediation table. They wait. Their eyes, like spotlights, are on the mediator. She begins. What is said and how the mediator begins informs the parties about what to expect in the mediation process and what to expect of the mediator. Of even more importance in the view of a mediator committed to the transformative approach, the mediator will use the opening moments to move out of the spotlights and shift them onto the participants. As a result, the parties are encouraged to take control of the process and begin productive work in the mediation within minutes of sitting down at the table as they and the mediator set the stage for their work together.

An opening statement is a component of all stage models of mediation and mediation training. Whether the training is for school peer mediation or commercial cases in civil courts, mediators learn an opening statement. Certain elements are common to all openings, and mediators are taught to:

- Explain the mediation process
- Describe the role of the mediator
- Discuss the goals of mediation
- Discuss "ground rules" or "behavioral guidelines"
- Explain confidentiality
- Describe caucus procedure
- Confirm commitment of the parties to the process

In addition, the opening statement is seen as serving multiple purposes, including putting the parties at ease, creating a conducive climate, gaining their commitment to mediate and establishing control of the process.

The transformative mediator will begin the mediation with consideration of these same elements, but he will examine closely his traditional opening statement for its assumptions about the parties and the goals of the mediator and the mediation process. The result is likely to be new descriptive content and a different mode of presentation.

Transformative mediators come to mediation believing that the people before them are capable of increasing their ability to deal with conflict and individual differences and of making the best decisions for themselves about what to do in their situation. They also believe that, given the opportunity, participants in mediation want to make their decisions taking into account the other's views and perspectives and are capable of consideration for the other even in the midst of conflict. Transformative mediators also believe that the participants are capable of deciding what kind of mediation process they want and will work best for them. Transformative mediators consider themselves facilitators of a discussion or conversation between individuals in conflict, rather than as an expert in negotiation, option generation, and resolutions. Mediators are there to be responsive to participants' needs, to focus on their statements in the conversation, to explore their meaning and to slow down at opportunities to encourage deliberation and decision-making and invite consideration of the other's perspective. All of these premises and beliefs will be reflected in the opening of the mediation.

Description of Mediation

In explaining the mediation process, a transformative mediator describes it as a forum for the parties to discuss all of their issues and concerns. **The mediator invites the parties to use the mediation to have a conversation about whatever is important to them.** No limits are placed on what will be appropriate for discussion or the way in which it is said. Talking about the past in an emotional way may be just what the parties want to do. If the mediator tells the parties directly or indirectly that some things are off limits (whether in opening the mediation or at any point in the process), the mediator is placing herself in a position of authority and disempowering the parties.

The mediator will not emphasize resolution as the only goal. Settlement is described as only one possible outcome among many. Others, which may be suggested by the mediator, include new or better understanding of the situation and of the other party, individual or joint understanding of new possibilities or options, and agreement about a new course of action. It may also be suggested that the parties may find that the concerns are no longer of concern as a result of the discussion.

What the mediator says may sound something like this:

Mediation gives you the opportunity to discuss all of the issues and concerns that have brought you here.

Mediation may help you as individuals to:
- Think about your goals
- Gather information needed
- Consider other resources
- Identify options open to you
- Hear and better understand the views and perspective of the other person at the table
- Decide what is important
- Choose a course of action that may be an agreement resolving the matter in a manner satisfactory to both of you or may be some other course of action. People often find all of these are valuable results of mediation, but you will be the best judge of what you want and find useful and valuable.

Mediation provides opportunities for the parties to make decisions. Decision-making takes place on many levels and certainly includes the decision to walk in the door and sit down. A party who did not take off her coat and refused to sit at the table, instead choosing to sit against the wall several feet from the table, was making a decision. At the completion of the opening statement the mediator invited her to sit at the table at that point by saying, "Would you like to join us?" and her move to the table was also a decision and a dramatic one sending an important message. Decisions also include deciding what to talk about, how to talk about it and whether to listen to the other party or not. Decisions arise at every moment in the process well before the decision of whether to agree on a particular proposed resolution or not. As each decision is made, each seemingly small, the empowerment effect is cumulative.

In describing mediation, the mediator may also explain that the process to be followed will be worked out by the parties with the help of the mediator. Since the mediator follows the parties, the mediator does not decide how the process works, but the parties talk about their concerns and then decide what they want to do next. For example, they will decide if they need more information before continuing the discussion, or they may want to simply propose solutions and bargain without further investigation or discussion. The mediator does not lead the parties from one "stage" of mediation to the next, but moves with them as they move through a process that makes sense to them. The mediator stays alert to what the parties are doing and the choice they have made by making observations to clarify with the parties what it is the mediator observes and checking in with them that this is what they want.

Role of the Mediator

Mediators discuss their role from the standpoint of the transformational goals of empowerment and recognition. They mention activities such as:

- Asking the parties what it is they wish to talk about, whether particular events, their feelings about the events or requests for the future;
- Listening to the parties, summarizing and asking questions;
- Assisting a party to talk about concerns, to listen and ask questions, and to understand the issues; and
- Assisting the parties with making choices about what to do about the situation.

They may describe their role as supportive of both parties and not directive. They do not direct the parties to any particular topics or outcomes. Instead they see their role as assisting the parties to become clearer about the issues and better able to decide what they want to do about them. They look for those empowerment opportunities to highlight for the parties. They also look for, and highlight, recognition opportunities to assist the parties to enhance communication and better understand each other.

It will be helpful if mediators are explicit about their belief that the parties know best what they wish to discuss and that only they can individually decide what they want to do. Of course, the mediators emphasize that they will not make any decisions for the parties or suggest any direction for them and will not try to persuade them to come to a settlement.

> I hope to assist you both to talk about your concerns and to fully understand the issues involved. I will be supportive of both of you and your goals. I will listen to you and ask questions, and you will also have the opportunity to listen and ask questions of each other. I will also assist you with considering your goals and choices, but I will not make any decisions for you. If you want to make any choices about what to do in this situation or to resolve it, the decision will be yours.

Goals of Mediation

Individuals in mediation may experience empowerment in mediation from the very first moments of the opening of mediation if that is the goal of the mediator and the mediator is sensitive to opportunities for decision-making. Telling a person that they will be empowered or that any decisions they make will be voluntary is not the same as the mediator actually behaving as though the mediator respected the ability of the individual to make decisions from the beginning of the mediation.

One significant step enabling a mediator to facilitate both empow-

erment and recognition is to ask the parties to talk about their goals for the mediation. The transformative mediator understands that the goals for the mediation must be the goals the parties have determined for themselves, individually and together, and that the goals will evolve and perhaps change as the mediation progresses. Rather than telling the parties what the goal of mediation should be, such as improving communication, reaching agreement and ending the conflict, the mediator asks the parties about their goals and hopes for the mediation.

Viewing the opening as part of the conversation with the parties about what brings them to mediation and what they hope to achieve allows an informal discussion with them about goals for mediation as a process before getting to specific substantive goals. The questions for the parties to think about are "Why are you interested in mediation?" and "What do you hope to accomplish by using mediation as a process?" Even though the mediator believes mediation would be good for the parties, an explanation by the mediator is not as powerful as the parties attempting to articulate their own reasons.

The first goal of the transformative mediator is a focus on empowerment. One form this takes is an increased capacity of the parties to understand and deal with their conflict. Helping the individuals to think about why they want to be in mediation enables them to understand for themselves why they are there and what might be possible for them. Involving the participants in thinking about their goals for mediation even at the beginning of the process is empowering. Even the response of "I don't know" is empowering, because it is likely to lead to further discussion and possible clarification. At the very least, that person and the other party know where they are and what they might be talking about first in the mediation.

The most empowering approach is to simply ask the participants to talk about their goals for using mediation:

> What you want to do in mediation is ultimately your choice. I want to give you a chance to talk about your purpose and goals for being here. Do you want to talk about your goals for mediation? What do you hope to accomplish with mediation? Why is that important to you?

Mediators are often not comfortable with such open-ended questions early in the process because, of course, the parties will begin to talk at this point, may refer to the issues that bring them to mediation and may even argue. Since the mediator follows the parties, if the parties talk about something else or start to tell their story, the mediator will be responsive to what is said rather than bring them back to the subject raised by the mediator.

For the mediator who is not ready to try the open-ended discussion, there are other ways of getting to the discussion of the participants' goals.

The mediator might offer assumptions about the parties' goals and check out those assumptions with them. Assumptions of the mediator can often be way off the mark. Mediators often assume, for example, that people wish to improve their communication, when what one person may want more than anything is to avoid having to communicate with the other in any way. But assumptions can be framed in a way that they would be hard to differ with. For example, the assumption that both parties want the conflict to end in a way that seems fair to both is a pretty safe assumption, and may educate the parties about a goal of the mediator. As such it is likely to be directive and not empowering.

Another less open ended and fearsome approach, although not as empowering, is offering a menu of possibilities, and asking if any of those possibilities is important to the parties.

> Did any of the things I described about mediation strike you as something you would like to see happen here? Such as: Discussing your concerns? Improving communication? Listening to each other? Gathering information? Thinking about your choices?

A follow up question could then elicit more personal information and concerns relevant to the individual.

> Why is that important to you?

Setting "Ground Rules"

"Ground rules" are often considered essential for an effective process and to create the environment for an orderly discussion in a rational and unemotional manner. Ground rules, the thinking goes, enable the mediator to try to enforce the kind of behavior many mediators consider most conducive to effective resolution. Yet most mediators are well aware that they are only trying to enforce the ground rules. Parties do not follow the best of ground rules, and setting ground rules puts the mediator in the role of enforcer of something that can rarely be enforced and is actually a distraction from what the parties may be trying to say. Enforcement of ground rules means the mediator and the other party may be missing some important points trying to be made. It also distorts the role of the mediator from that of facilitator of the conversation to controlling the process. The mediator may be missing opportunities to increase empowerment by failing to highlight decision points for the parties.

It is quite another matter if the parties request certain ground rules and agree to them in advance or at a point when it becomes apparent that they would be helpful. This approach is empowering. Then the mediator is not an enforcer, but is assisting the parties with decision-making about the kind of process they want. If they set the ground rules, but are not following them, the mediator will remind them that they requested certain guidelines for discussion. So, rather than enforcing ground rules, the mediator will suggest a discussion with the parties of their difficulties with them and whether they still want to try to observe them or do something else. Here the process still belongs to the parties and they are making the decisions about it. This is empowerment.

If the mediator asks the parties if they would like to suggest any guidelines for the discussions, it puts them in charge, where they should be, and is empowering for both. It also provides opportunities for recognition as new information may be shared. They may have special issues that will not be covered in the mediator's "one size fits all" guidelines. A man may ask that the woman not cry, or the woman that the man not raise his voice. There is no requirement that the rules cover both of them. If the woman isn't sure she can avoid crying, some discussion of what they want to do in case it happens, or is about to, is also empowering because they will discover that they have choices in dealing with behavior. In addition, the effort to accommodate each other opens up recognition opportunities as they come to understand the effect of particular behavior on the other. The mediator may initiate this discussion with a question such as "What if you find you must cry?" The woman may agree to ask for a break, or the man may agree to ignore it or to leave the room briefly. Once a plan is in place the impact of any crying, or the man leaving the room, will be very different because it is being done by choice and by agreement.

> Many people I work with have already tried to discuss the situation, but found they got stuck. This is an opportunity for you to talk about the situation in a new way if that is what you want. Sometimes guidelines for your conversation here in mediation can be helpful in accomplishing that. Do you have any requests or suggestions for discussion guidelines that you think would be helpful to make things go better for you here?

If the participants have no idea about what you are talking about, it is helpful to offer some suggestions.

> For example, some people want to know the other is really listening and want to be able to talk without being interrupted. Is that something you want?

The response is likely to be, "No, thank you." Many parties invited to set discussion guidelines will say they have no need for them. If you have asked and that is the response, the mediator must then respect the answer. It is helpful, however, to point out that discussion guidelines may be raised by either of them or by the mediator at any time. How the discussion is going for them is just as important as what is being discussed. Asking the parties for their permission to raise the issue of how the discussion is going at any time you think it would be helpful in the context of a particular discussion is consistent with the role of the transformative mediator.

> As I work with you I might observe some ways of interacting that seem to interfere with your reaching the goals you said you want to accomplish. Would you like me to comment on those if I do observe anything I think could be helpful? You both may also wish to observe and comment about the interactions as we go along or ask questions. Do either of you have any observation or requests of me or the other now?

The party who said: "No rules will keep me from yelling or insulting him if things get a little hot" was stating a truism about mediation and parties in conflict and about herself in particular. In this case, the other party suggested proceeding without guidelines, but if either felt the need for one, he or she would suggest it as they went along. These parties were already acting from a place of empowerment and recognition early in the process of mediation. This kind of interaction and process discussion sets the stage or lays a foundation for the discussions of substance that are to follow.

Mediators who have been taught to establish ground rules and to enforce them may find the prospect of simply going ahead with no rules (if the parties so choose) somewhat unnerving. An initial small step for that mediator in the direction of encouraging the parties to set their own rules is to move away from simply laying out the rules to more party focus. Explain the reasons for any rules you believe you must have. If you want to enforce the rule of "no interruptions", explain why. "Since it is important that each of you try to understand the other's point of view, you will need to listen carefully to each other. I ask that each of you not interrupt when the other is talking." OR "You said you want an agreement that will meet both your needs. I suggest it will be helpful for you to listen carefully to what you each want, and not interrupt." OR "You may be asking the other to do something to resolve this matter. It would be helpful if you did not insult each other if you want the other to cooperate with you."

Another somewhat larger step toward party empowerment in the area of discussion guidelines is to ask for their agreement to any rules you desire. "Since you want to improve your communication, it is important that each of you listen carefully to each other. I ask that each of you not interrupt when the other is talking. Are you willing to do that?" If the answer is no, of course the mediator must respect the answer, or, if the mediator can't accept it, discuss some other variation that will partially meet the mediator's needs, such as "Are you willing to try to listen and not interrupt?"

Note, however, that the focus here has shifted from the parties' choices to the mediators need for particular ground rules. **Also keep in mind that** some standard ground rules, such as no interruptions, are based in the view of one cultural model of how conversations and discussions should take place. Loud and interactive conversations may signal interest and involvement, not rude interruptions, to many people. Imposing rules of behavior is not only difficult and disempowering, it may also be disrespectful on the part of the mediator.

Confidentiality

> I am committed to keeping everything you say here confidential. No one out-side this room will hear about what you say from me. What are your expectations or requests relating to confidentiality?

Be prepared for surprises and to follow. Even something as basic of confidentiality may lead to discussion and disagreement between the parties.

Caucus

> There may come a time when you may be more comfortable talking to me privately without the other party in the room. You may have something you want to talk through or questions to ask. I may also want to suggest we meet privately if I think it would be helpful. Either of you may request a pri-vate meeting at any time, or I may do so. If I meet privately with one of you, of course I will also meet with the other. You will decide whether what we talk about in our private meetings will be confidential or shared with the other party.

The caucus is a valuable part of the mediation process for promoting the purposes of empowerment and recognition. Assisting one party to think through an issue or proposal, to consider goals, resources, choices and possi-ble results is furthering the goal of empowerment. Recognition is also possible when a party may consider new information and whether to trust that information or new understanding it might suggest about the other party. A party may also want to discuss some aspect of himself that he is not ready to put forward in a joint meeting. The mediator may also act as a sounding board or coach for the party who is not sure how to put forward a proposal or share information. The caucus is obviously not the time to now drop the goals of empowerment and recognition and tell the parties what they should do or push for settlement. The goals of empowerment and recognition must guide the actions of the mediator even when out of scrutiny of the other party.

Commitment to the Process

Good. You have done some important work here already. You have goals
you hope to achieve in mediation and talked about some guidelines for your
discussions. As we go along you may want to review and reconsider those
and that is just fine. Also you want things to happen here, and we can't pre-
dict now just what will happen. I would ask you to be open to see what
happens and give yourself time to let your ideas percolate as you relflect
about what's happening and what you are hearing. It is your choice whether
you want to proceed with mediation. Are you prepared to go ahead with
mediation as we have discussed it?

Design the Process

What usually happens now is that each of you has a chance to talk about
your concerns, and after we have spent some time talking about them, we
could consider together what steps you want to take then. You may want·to
talk about options and choices you have. You may want to gather more
information. Would you want to start with talking about why you are here? .
. . Is that OK with you? . . . You both will have as much time as you need.
Who would like to start?

Again, party choice is presented. What if they don't agree? What if they
don't like your idea? That's fine, what do they want to do. What if they can't
decide who should start? What do they want to do? Is this the time to have
an argument? It is amazing what can happen when control is turned over to
the parties. They have ideas. One may say he doesn't need to hear a statement from the other, but has some questions for him. The other may say
fine, go ahead and ask. And the mediation is under way. Not in the way the
mediator would design it, but in a way the parties want to start. With the
mediator's role of following the parties, but observing the interactions and
process, the mediator will check in as the process moves along to see if it still
works for both parties. The parties will give the mediator clues if it is not
working, and the mediator will ask them.

Since the mediator does not have a rigid view of how the process should
begin and progress, there is no one right way to start. Parties may want to start
with a response to a written proposal sent before the mediation started. Parties
may just want to talk with each other without formal opening statements from
each, or they may like the idea of a formal statement. The mediator has in mind
a "mental map" of the kinds of activities the parties are likely to engage in, but
are not required in any particular series of stages. Instead the flow of the mediation goes as the parties' needs take them. If ground rules are not set in the

beginning, they may come up later if one party feels continuously insulted by the other, for example. If information is not shared at the beginning, it may be shared when the need for it makes it apparent.

Conclusion

Interestingly, if the mediator can step out of the way, opening up the "opening" of the mediation to party participation and even control facilitates the flow of the mediation and enhances the decision-making capabilities of the parties throughout the process. It is also interesting to note that with some participants and a skilled and confident transformative mediator, some or all of the usual components of an "opening" may simply become irrelevant. A mediator who is following the parties and turning over control of the topics for discussion to the parties may find that they have no interest in, and no need for, a formal "opening" of the mediation. The participants may quickly interrupt the opening process with their own questions and issues in conflict, and the mediation then begins in the way the parties take it. The potential empowerment that results from this first response on the part of the mediator is significant and each such moment builds party strength over the course of the mediation. These mediator moves, deriving from the beliefs underlying transformative mediation, will result in the abandonment of an opening statement conducted by ticking off the points on an opening statement checklist. This mediator, rather than following the recipe or guidebook for an opening statement, truly signals the work of a creative transformative mediator and the beginning of a successful mediation.

NINE

Recognition in Theory, Practice and Training

By Dorothy J. Della Noce

Understanding the concepts of empowerment and recognition is fundamental to the theory and practice of the transformative framework. Of the
two, I have found that recognition is the more challenging for mediators to
grasp, in training as well as in practice. I believe that this is because certain
aspects of the concept of recognition are at once comfortably familiar and
disturbingly foreign to mediators and mediation trainees.

In this chapter I elaborate the concept of recognition in the context of
some of the confusion that has grown up around it since the term was first
introduced to the mediation field (Bush, 1989; Bush and Folger, 1994). My
goal is to help mediators gain clarity on what recognition is and is not, and to
help trainers effectively develop with trainees a clear sense of the premises
and practice of recognition. I will begin by reviewing Bush and Folger's definition of recognition and situating recognition in the theoretical framework
of transformative practice. I will then address the most common sources of
confusion surrounding the concept of recognition, including some definitional confusion, concerns that the goal of fostering recognition makes
mediation a (foreign) therapeutic process, and the impression that recognition
is an element of the (familiar) practice of interest-based bargaining. I close
with some suggestions on how to develop further clarity on recognition, in
practice and in training.

Recognition in the Transformative Framework

The transformative framework for mediation practice emerges from a
theory of conflict transformation, embedded in a relational view of the world
(Bush and Folger, 1994). In this paradigm, conflict is a crisis in human interaction that generates particular human responses: relative weakness and
self-absorption (Bush and Folger, 1994). Yet, within this crisis lie opportunities for individual and interactional growth and change ("transformation") in
two dimensions of human experience: empowerment and recognition (Bush

and Folger, 1994). Empowerment and recognition each embody a particular dynamic of interaction. The dynamic of empowerment involves incremental changes in the parties' sense of personal strength and ability to take control of their own situation, while the dynamic of recognition involves incremental changes in the capacity for interpersonal understanding (Bush and Folger, 1994).

Although there is a constant interplay between empowerment and recognition, the focus of this chapter is on recognition. **The hallmark of recognition is letting go of one's exclusive focus on oneself and becoming interested in the perspective of another** (Bush and Folger, 1994), **which is also known as** *cognitive empathy* **or** *perspective-taking* (Della Noce, 1999). That is, because conflict confronts a party with a person in a different situation, who holds a contrary viewpoint, it provides an opportunity for a party to try to appreciate and acknowledge the perspective of another (Bush and Folger, 1994).

Sources of Confusion Regarding Recognition

Bush and Folger's transformative framework has had an interesting reception in the mediation field. The concept of empowerment was easily accommodated, probably because the mediation field has a history of honoring, at least in rhetoric if not always in practice, principles of party autonomy and self-determination. References to empowerment, autonomy or self-determination appear in various practice handbooks, standards of conduct for mediators, and even training standards. Even though the concept of empowerment can be defined and understood somewhat differently by different mediators (see, e.g., Cobb, 1993), and is sometimes confused with the idea of power balancing, it is nonetheless widely regarded as an accepted component of competent mediation practice (Shailor, 1994).

Recognition, on the other hand, is not as deeply embedded in the history and literature of the mediation field. Mediation texts that predate *The Promise of Mediation* give no noticeable attention to recognition. Nor does fostering inter-party recognition appear in the standards of practice or training standards of any major mediation organization. Perhaps this is because recognition is a fundamentally relational concept and practice (Della Noce, 1999), and relational premises have just begun to emerge in the mediation field in the last decade. In fact, as will be discussed in more detail below, it seems to me that a great deal of the confusion which has grown up around the concept of recognition springs from attempts to fit this relational concept to familiar individualist assumptions.

Through my experience as a trainer, and in reviewing the literature in the field, I categorize common sources of confusion regarding the concept of recognition as follows: (1) defining recognition, (2) distinguishing the practice of fostering recognition from therapy, and (3) distinguishing the practice of fostering recognition from interest-based bargaining. I address each of these separately in the sections that follow.

Definitional Problems: What Kind of Empathy - and Between Whom?

Empathy is a complex concept with a number of different meanings. Duan and Hill (1996) try to simplify this complexity by distinguishing two core categories of empathy: *affective empathy* (or *empathic emotions*), responding to another's emotion with the same emotion, and *cognitive empathy*, intellectually taking the perspective of another. They propose that affective empathy and cognitive empathy exist as distinct phenomena, while also acknowledging that the cognitive and affective elements of empathy very likely influence each other in ways not yet known. This concept of two different "kinds" of empathy is useful for understanding the nature of recognition.

Efforts by a mediator to support recognition in the mediation interaction are situated within the cognitive, rather than affective, dimension of empathy (Della Noce, 1999). **That is, in fostering recognition, the mediator's attention is on helping the parties step into each other's worlds, understand each other's situations, experiences, limitations and perspectives, and create shared meaning** (Bush and Folger, 1994; Della Noce, 1999). While the parties may experience an affective response to this growing cognitive understanding, the mediator is not attempting to create or provoke an affective response in either party. The mediator's goal is to help the parties understand. See Figure 1.

Figure 1: Categories of Empathy

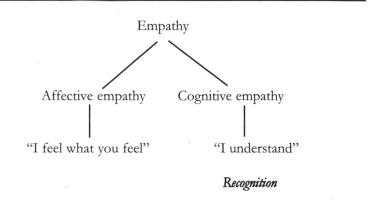

Overlooking this distinction between cognitive and affective empathy appears to have created confusion for critics like Menkel-Meadow (1995), who understands empathy in the mediation context to be "asking [the parties] to feel for and with each other," and who thereby collapses the expression of feelings with recognition. It could also explain two related phenomena: the perception that the transformative framework is appropriate only for cases in which people need to "talk about their feelings," and the perception that the mediator working from transformative premises regularly asks the parties, "How do you feel about that?"

With recognition understood as cognitive empathy, both of these perceptions are revealed as ill-founded. We see that the appropriateness of mediation from the transformative framework is not limited to cases where parties need to talk about feelings, but includes all cases where the conflict interaction between the people involved - how the individuals are relating to each other in the midst of conflict - can benefit from the improved interpersonal understanding of the recognition dimension (as well as the increased clarity and decision-making capacity that emerge from the empowerment dimension).

Moreover, we see that in the transformative orientation, while the question "How do you feel about that?" may be appropriate at times, there are also times when it may be terribly inappropriate and intrusive and a mediator would not think to ask it. The question itself, taken out of context, is not indicative of whether or not a mediator is working from transformative premises. Rather, it is whether the question is appropriately responsive, at that moment, to an opportunity to develop interpersonal understanding that is emerging in the parties' own conversation. In other words, if the parties' raise the topic of feelings somehow in their own conversation, and if it appears that it opens an opportunity for increased cognitive understanding between the parties, the mediator will follow that cue, respond to it, and invite the parties' to elaborate. But if those conditions are not present, it is not appropriate for the mediator to open an unsolicited exploration of the parties' feelings.

This approach treats emotional expression as part of the ongoing, purposeful communication between the parties. The mediator working from transformative premises attends to the parties' expressions of emotion (as he or she does with all of the parties' communication) for the opportunities they present for developing greater interpersonal understanding and personal clarity through dialogue (Bush and Folger, 1994; Folger and Bush, 1996; Della Noce, 1999). Note that this provides the mediator with a different frame for responding to the parties' emotional expression than is found in problem-solving models of mediation, which suggest that emotional expression is an impediment to rational discussion and the goal of settlement, and therefore the mediator must deal with emotional expression by circumscribing it in advance through ground rules, ignoring it, "allowing" a one-sided "venting" process, suppressing it, reframing it, and otherwise limiting or controlling it.

Moreover, noting these differences actually highlights another important point regarding the parties' emotional expression. Apparently, at some level, the parties in most mediations (no matter what the mediator's framework) do indeed indicate a "need to talk about their feelings." If emotional expression were not an inherent and expected part of conflict interactions, I doubt that we would see so many pages of text, in so many books and training manuals, dedicated to advising the mediator on how to control or otherwise deal with the parties' emotional expression. The difference between transformative and problem-solving models lies in the ideologically-based assumptions about the role of emotions that each model supports, and therefore the mediators' different theoretical framework for understanding and responding to the parties' (inevitable) expressions of emotion.

The next level of confusion I have observed regarding recognition involves who provides recognition during the interaction. I first encountered this confusion at a training program in which I was playing the mediator in a role play demonstration. In the course of debriefing the role play, several trainees expressed surprise that I did not "acknowledge" the parties. Discussion revealed that the trainees understood "recognition" as the mediator showing empathy toward each of the parties. While references to this kind of mediator-to-party empathy appear in some of the literature in the field, as well as some training standards, it is not recognition. **Recognition consists of empathy between the parties, not empathy from a mediator to a party.** It is the developing empathy between the parties that holds transformative potential: the potential for change in the conflict interaction. Mediator-to-party empathy serves different purposes, which I believe have more to do with interpersonal influence (Della Noce, 1999). In fact, Duan & Hill (1996) refer to professional-to-client empathy as "therapeutic empathy."

In summary, regarding the definitional confusion which has grown up around recognition, this analysis should clarify that **the mediator intervenes, not to generate an affective response in a party, or to offer his or her own understanding to either party, but to encourage cognitive perspective-taking *between* the parties, in order to help them develop better understandings of one another.**

But, it is the mediator's goal of fostering the development of inter-party cognitive empathy (the other goal being to foster party empowerment) that raises another source of confusion some have expressed: is a process which has interpersonal understanding as one of its goals properly called mediation, or is it more accurately described as counseling or therapy? This will be discussed in the next section.

Recognition as a Goal: Is It Still Mediation?

Scholars and practitioners have struggled for years to define mediation as a unique social practice, distinct from therapy, the practice of law, arbitration, adjudication and judicial settlement conferences. As a consequence, mediation is often defined as much by what it is *not* as by what it *is*.

One of the most perplexing boundary issues - for all approaches to mediation - has been that between mediation and therapy (see, e.g., Brown, 1988; Folberg and Taylor, 1984; Haynes, 1992; Haynes, 1994; Haynes and Haynes, 1989; Kelly, 1983; Milne and Folberg, 1988; and Roberts, 1992). The traditional position on this issue has been to distinguish mediation from therapeutic interventions in terms of the goal of a settlement agreement. According to this view, as long as the *mediator* has the goal of producing a tangible settlement agreement, the process is mediation, even in those cases where the mediator uses the techniques and interventions of a therapist (see, e.g., Benjamin, 1998; Brown, 1988; Haynes, 1992; Haynes and Haynes, 1989; Kelly, 1983).

Making the distinction in this way has never been entirely satisfactory. A number of commentators describe the distinction as difficult and elusive (see, e.g., comments by Milne and Folberg, 1988; Benjamin, 1998). It also raises as many questions as it tries to answer. For example, since judicial settlement conferences have the goal of settlement, are they thereby the equivalent of mediation? What about those forms of therapy that include agreement as a goal? What about an approach where the mediator alternates goals between therapy and settlement (e.g., Irving and Benjamin, 1995)?

Bush & Folger (1994) called the adequacy of the traditional "distinction" between mediation and therapy into question when they introduced the theory and practice of the transformative framework, and argued that empowerment and recognition, not settlement alone, are the goals of the mediation process. Their work has also raised a more fundamental issue: is the goal of settlement the hallmark of the mediation process? In the next sections, I address whether settlement must be a hallmark of the mediation process, and propose an alternative approach to distinguishing mediation from therapy.

The Goal of Settlement

For some authors, it is inconceivable that mediation could be separated from the goal of settlement. Huber (in press) provides a fairly typical example. He claims that "seeking a settlement is the essence of mediation." Since settlement is not the *mediator's* goal in the transformative framework (note that it *could* still be the goal of one or both of the parties), Huber has no framework for understanding this process as mediation, and so he dismisses it as therapeutic.

What this argument misses is that the settlement-driven definition of mediation is bound in a particular (problem-solving) theory of conflict resolution, which is embedded in even more fundamental ideological assumptions about the nature of human beings and the social world. It thereby misses the socially-constructed nature of this particular definition of mediation, that is, that this definition does not reflect any necessary objective reality about the essential nature of mediation, but only the fact that some mediators and scholars, historically, have chosen to define mediation in this way. This definition is logical, and even necessary, in the individualist framework, because of the underlying assumptions that conflict represents a competition for scarce resources or a problem in individual needs-satisfaction between fundamentally self-interested human beings. No other definition makes sense in that framework, given those assumptions.

But, relational views of human nature and conflict, and relational approaches to conflict resolution, are being explored by scholars from a number of disciplines (see, e.g., Bush and Folger, 1994; Deetz and White, 1999; Folger and Bush, 1994; Gray, 1994; Greenhalgh, 1995; Koehn, 1998; Kolb and Putnam, 1997; McNamee and Gergen, 1999; Pearce and Littlejohn, 1997; Putnam, 1994). Many of these scholars embrace the idea of third party intervention in conflict, but envision a different role for the third party, and different goals of intervention, than individualist assumptions and problem-solving theories allow. In the relational worldview, assumptions of the fundamentally social human being and the primacy of dialogic interaction open possibilities for theory and practice that cannot be contemplated from another point of view.

The transformative framework emerges from this relational worldview and therefore provides new insights on the process of mediation, and alternative constructions of the roles and goals of the parties and the mediator. The process is still mediation, but it is informed with relational sensibilities. And, as I have argued elsewhere, it is more constructive for mediators and scholars to develop clarity on the differences in theoretical frameworks, and the different ideological assumptions from which they emerge, than to argue that one framework or another represents "real" mediation (Della Noce, 1999).

But what about the specific question regarding the boundaries between mediation and therapy? I address this in the next section.

Mediation and Therapy

For years mediators have instinctively recoiled at the suggestion that their practices might be considered therapy. In fact, Bush and Folger (1994) describe the mediation field as "hypersensitive" in this regard. This has led to the sort of verbal gymnastics whereby mediators tout the therapeutic effects of mediation, and defend their use of therapeutic techniques, all the while trying to distance their activities from those of therapy. (At the same time, I have often wondered why mediators are hypersensitive to the boundaries between mediation and therapy, yet appear less concerned with the boundaries between mediation and such processes as the practice of law, arbitration, and adjudication.)

I believe the question about the boundaries between mediation and therapy is, at one level, a very general question about the boundaries of mediation per se, and at another level, it reflects concern with empathy as a goal of mediation. What I will do in this section is point out where and how I believe it is possible to draw boundaries between mediation and other social processes, acknowledge that situations may arise in which the boundaries are not so clear, and discuss how this might be approached in the future.

First, I propose that the key to distinguishing mediation from therapy - and from any other social practice, for that matter lies in an analysis and comparison of both the *theory* and *discursive practice* of each process. This allows me to readily identify a rather clear boundary between most of what goes by the name of therapy and the transformative framework for mediation.

First, at the level of fundamental assumptions, many therapeutic theories and practices build on and embody individualist assumptions (Doherty, 1998). Although "therapy" encompasses a sweeping array of theories and practices, many therapeutic theories are concerned with diagnosis and therapeutic treatment or remediation of individual *diseases and disorders*, whether physical, mental or behavioral.

In contrast, the theory of conflict upon which the transformative approach is based embodies relational, rather than individualist assumptions. Moreover, transformative theory does not consider conflict to be a disease or disorder, and does not suggest the need for either diagnosis or treatment of the individuals involved. **Mediators using the transformative framework are not attempting to heal or cure anyone. In fact, mediators driven by the goal of healing are most likely practicing problem-solving mediation, the twist being that they have defined the "problem" in therapeutic terms.** (To see this difference quite clearly, compare the transformative framework with Irving and Benjamin (1995), which presents an interest-based, problem-solving model of mediation embedded in therapeu-

103

tic theory and based on both diagnosis and treatment of the parties by the mediator.)

On the other hand, as the relational worldview on which the transformative framework rests continues to develop, emerging theories of therapeutic practice based on this worldview may bear some resemblance to theories of conflict transformation, because they will be based on similar values, and similar views of human beings and social interaction (see generally, McNamee and Gergen, 1999, for an exploration of relational values and the corresponding orientations toward a variety of social practices). Thus, theory alone may not be a sufficient marker of the distinctions between social practices.

Therefore, I suggest that whether a mediator is engaged in the same process as a therapist will depend on an empirical comparison of the discourse markers of each practice. Through discourse analytic research, we will be able to examine whether mediators and therapists interact with their clients in the same way, with the same goals. In this way we can build a grounded understanding of how mediation and other social practices based on the relational worldview may be similar and different, and then consider what that means. In the meantime, I suggest that we exchange hypersensitivity for genuine curiosity, and open exploration of this question in ways it has not been opened in the past.

Empathy as a Goal

One reason the transformative framework, in particular, seems to provoke questions about the boundaries between mediation and therapy, appears to be that recognition is made a goal of the process. Moore, for example, describes fostering recognition as "more akin to therapeutic or group dynamic interventions" than to mediation (1996). Similarly, Slaikeu (1996) suggests that his model of integrative mediation should be distinguished from "other processes such as counseling, psychotherapy, family therapy, and spiritual direction that have as their primary focus awareness/empowerment and understanding/recognition."

Yet, we know from research that cognitive empathy has been associated with enhanced process and outcomes in conflict interactions (see, e.g, Falk and Johnson, 1977; Kemp and Smith, 1994; Neale and Bazerman, 1983; Richardson, Hammock, Smith, Gardner and Signo, 1994; Sessa, 1996). In mediation specifically, Slaikeu, Pearson and Thoennes (1988) found that there were more empathic statements between spouses in successful cases than in unsuccessful cases, and even recommended that mediators be "proactive" in encouraging perspective-taking between parties.

If inter-party cognitive empathy has demonstrated value for conflict, then creating an environment in which empathy is supported should be an *objective*, not just an accident, of mediation (Bush and Folger, 1994; Bush, 1996). And doing so does not change the process from the third party conflict intervention of mediation into therapy. As Broome (1993) points out in his argument for greater attention to empathy in conflict theory, while empathy is an important aspect of counseling, psychology and psychotherapy, it is also crucial to communication, sociology, social inquiry and methodology, and philosophy. Duan and Hill (1996) make the point more expansively, noting that "empathy is the very basis of *all human interaction*." (My emphasis.)

To equate supporting the development of interpersonal cognitive empathy with the practice of therapy not only ignores what we know about the value of cognitive empathy for conflict interactions, it also suggests that only therapists may help human beings understand each other. If such is the case, then we have no basis for conflict resolution, or family life, or diplomacy, or even constructive communication itself, absent therapist intervention. Therefore, I reject the premise that only therapists may properly engage in activities that help human beings build better interpersonal understanding.

Paradoxically, however, when the importance of fostering empathy in mediation is framed in this way, another question arises: namely, whether building understanding isn't precisely what occurs in interest based bargaining.

Isn't Recognition Just Interest-Based Bargaining?

Some have suggested that fostering recognition is part of the problem-solving model. For example, Slaikeu (1996) rejects recognition as a proper goal of the mediation process but then argues that, as a technique, recognition is simply a useful building block of problem-solving mediation, the functional equivalent of acknowledging the other side's interests in interest-based bargaining. Similarly, Menkel-Meadow (1995) says: "I feel compelled to add that I probably did not see anything new here because I do not see facilitating empathetic communication as 'new' or separate from problem-solving mediation." At one level, both authors are correct in noting that fostering inter-party understanding is an element of the problem-solving as well as the transformative frameworks. But the discussion needs to move to a deeper level, and consider how inter-party empathy, like other aspects of the mediation process, is shaped by theoretical frameworks embedded in ideological assumptions.

I have argued elsewhere that the concept and practice of empathy in the individualist paradigm of problem-solving mediation (which typically incorporates interest-based bargaining) is fundamentally different from that in the relational paradigm of conflict transformation, because each paradigm is based on different assumptions about the nature of human beings, how and why they relate to each other, and the nature and goals of interpersonal communication (Della Noce, 1999).

Problem-solving mediators foster *transactional empathy* between the parties: understanding between the parties is pursued and supported as an instrument of the transaction, and as a commodity to be exchanged, but not as a discrete goal of the process or an independently valued effect (Della Noce, 1999). **Transformative mediators foster relational empathy between the parties: inter-party understanding is considered an ongoing dialogic process, a goal of interaction in itself, and an independently valued effect of mediation** (Della Noce, 1999). See Figure 2.

Figure 2: Effects of worldviews on empathy

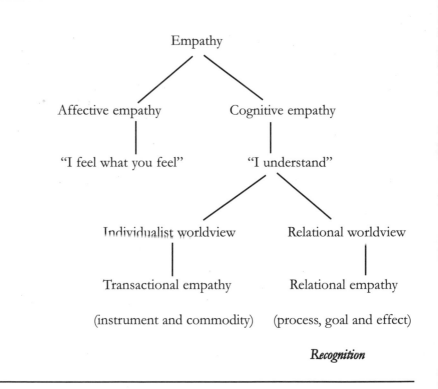

In practice, these different paradigms dispose mediators to attend to different conversational cues as opportunities for interpersonal understanding, highlight different aspects of the parties' conversations, and respond in distinctly different ways (see illustrations in Della Noce, 1999). These differences are evident from the very opening of the mediation. For example, **the relationally-oriented mediator is likely to frame improved interpersonal understanding as both a goal of the process and a valuable outcome in itself in the opening comments** (Folger and Bush, 1996). This frame, in turn, establishes and delimits a different range of opportunities for empathy in mediation practice than individualist ideology permits. Throughout the process, the relationally-oriented mediator maintains a micro-focus on interaction, and thereby attends to cues from the parties about how they want to be understood and how they are understanding the other and their situation. **The mediator fully expects the parties' emerging interpersonal understandings to be open, shifting and tentative, and therefore the mediator's interventions will support exploration and reflection, geared toward opening and encouraging dialogue and the development of shared meaning in discourse** (Della Noce, 1999).

A mediator who is focused on managing interest-based bargaining between the parties will not frame the mediation interaction in the same way, nor attend to the same cues, nor respond in the same way, as a mediator who is practicing from the transformative framework.

Implications for Training and Practice

Several implications emerge from this analysis that should be useful for mediators as well as trainers. These are listed here in the form of suggestions for those who are exploring, learning, or conducting training programs in the transformative framework. Many of these suggestions have been incorporated by Bush, Folger, Della Noce and Pope (1998) in *Advanced Mediation Skills for Postal Service Mediators: Practice within a Transformative Framework*, a program we designed and delivered for the United States Postal Service REDRESSTM mediation program.

Appreciate the Influence of Ideologies and Theories of Practice

Practices, such as fostering recognition between the parties, do not exist in a social vacuum. They cannot be separated from the mediator's fundamental assumptions about human beings and human interaction, or the theories of practice that are based on those assumptions (Della Noce, 1999). Both mediators and mediation trainers should develop an appreciation of the influence of ideologies and theories of practice. This can be accomplished by exploring the growing literature concerning the influence of ideologies on various social practices. This requires mediators to move beyond basic skills-oriented training programs, and into seminars or even local discussion groups that encourage study, dialogue and reflection. Bibliographies of relevant literature, such as those found in this volume and through the Institute for the Study of Conflict Transformation at Hofstra University School of Law, www.hofstra.edu/Law/isct, provide a good starting place.

Build Opportunities to Experience and Observe Recognition in Action

The power of recognition for changing a conflict interaction is best understood when mediators can connect with it on a personal level. For example, in training, we sometimes ask trainees to reflect on conflicts in which they have been personally involved, in which something powerful and positive happened, no matter what the outcome. As they share their stories, and describe what made the experience valuable and powerful, they typically describe recognition experiences such as discovering new insights and building new understandings.

Popular films provide another way to connect with the experience of recognition. It can be an interesting exercise for a mediator to watch conflict emerge and develop in the course of a film, and to analyze whether and how recognition is playing a part in the transformation of the conflict. As I developed this habit, I also developed a list of favorite film clips that provide a picture of recognition in action. Viewing clips like these with other mediators in small study groups fosters reflection and discussion about the moment-to-moment changes in conflict interaction and how those changes occur.

Provide Opportunities to Practice

Mediators in training should be given ample practice in working with recognition throughout the process: framing recognition as a goal and a valuable outcome in the opening comments, recognizing the opportunities for recognition that appear in the parties' conversational cues, creating responses that support the development of empathy, and summarizing and recording moments of recognition as an accomplishment of the mediation session if the parties so desire.

These dimensions of mediation are best practiced in small steps, which simultaneously reinforces the value of "micro-focus." (Although many of my comments here will encompass both empowerment and recognition, if your focus is on recognition, the exercises can be adjusted accordingly.)

Regarding openings, for example, after there has been discussion of the premises and goals of the transformative approach, I ask trainees to work alone for a time on developing an opening that reflects these goals and values. I then ask the trainees to break into pairs, and engage their partners in the "opening conversation" they have prepared. Partners critique the opening for how well it embodies and supports both empowerment and recognition, and then the trainees switch roles and repeat the exercise. Trainees discuss their impressions of the exercise, and often edit their opening remarks to take into account the feedback from their partners. Trainees return to the large group with two or three insights they gained from this exercise on how to open a mediation. Another variation on this exercise that I sometimes use is to provide the trainees with copies of a "scripted" opening statement and ask them to critique it, and reconstruct it, from the transformative framework. This same exercise can be done with Agreement to Mediate forms, which many mediators use in their practices. I sometimes distribute copies of forms I used (long ago) for this purpose.

As for practice in recognizing opportunities, I have found it most useful to do a particular variation of a demonstration role play for this purpose. I schedule this role play after there has been an introductory segment on how to identify the opportunities for empowerment and recognition that arise in the parties' own conversation. I frame in advance that the goal of this role play is to focus on opportunities, which means I am asking the trainees to pay attention to what the *parties* say, rather than what the mediator says. (In many cases I videotape the role play so we can return to it later to analyze the mediator's moves.) I distribute two sets of large colored cards to the trainees, one color bearing the word "Empowerment" and another the word "Recognition." I ask the trainees to hold up their cards whenever they detect an opportunity for either empowerment or recognition in what the parties say. As the role play proceeds, I make a number of stops, either to discuss an opportunity that a trainee has "flagged" with his or her card, or to highlight an opportunity that was not flagged and discuss why it might have been missed. Mediators can do a variation of this "flagging" exercise with commercial training videotapes, either in a self-study process or by working together with other mediators.

Another way to practice identifying opportunities for recognition is to work with small segments of transcribed discourse from mediations, and mine them for opportunities. I usually do this first as a group exercise via newsprint or an overhead projection, and then break the group into smaller workgroups to continue the exercise themselves.

Mediators can build on these same exercises to practice responding to opportunities for empowerment and recognition. For example, after an instructional segment on how to respond, I replay the videotape of the demonstration role play. The trainees have already practiced identifying opportunities using this mediation, so I shift the focus to noting and critiquing how the mediator responds, and how those responses capture (or miss) opportunities for empowerment and recognition. This exercise provides an excellent opportunity to reinforce the differences between mediator-to-party empathy and party-to-party empathy, as well as the differences between transactional and relational empathy.

Returning to the transcribed excerpts of mediation discourse, it can be very helpful to have the last few lines of transcription present an opportunity for recognition, and invite the trainees to discuss a number of different ways in which the mediator might respond to those opportunities.

Mediators should also practice responding in-the-moment to opportunities for empowerment and recognition through role plays. However, I seldom ask trainees to spend an hour or more independently role-playing, as has been customary in many of the trainings I have attended. I believe it is important that trainees be assisted in maintaining the micro-focus, and getting a sense of the contingency of each move made in the mediation, and that intensive coaching with a focus on the moment-to-moment discourse is essential. For these reasons, I use different role play formats that allow for frequent "analytical breaks" and discussion.

Focus on Interaction Rather than Psychology

A very important aspect of developing an understanding of recognition arises in the context of all of the exercises described in the prior subsection. As was explained earlier in this chapter, and elsewhere (Della Noce, 1999), fostering recognition requires a focus on dialogic interaction. **In coaching exercises and role plays with an eye toward recognition, it is important to maintain this interactional focus and be alert for the pull of psychological assumptions.** Watch for, and call attention to, psychological references by trainees, such as references to what parties "really mean" or "really want," or what a party's "hidden interest" is. I draw out discussion about these assumptions, asking trainees to talk about how they know what a party really means or what is hidden and when it is uncovered. And, I push trainees to focus on the dialogue, and work with what the parties are actually saying.

Along these same lines, mediators and trainers should be aware of the metaphors and images they use, whether in interaction with the parties or in training. With respect to fostering the interpersonal cognitive empathy of recognition, metaphors and images of voice, conversation, music and dance

110

emphasize this interactive focus (see, e.g., Burkitt, 1999; Lannaman, 1999).

Conclusion

In summary, I hope this chapter contributes to greater clarity about the concept of recognition, some sources of confusion that have grown up around it, and how to develop facility with the practice of fostering recognition in a mediation.

TEN

Identifying Opportunities
for Empowerment and Recognition in Mediation

**By Janet Kelly Moen, Donna Turner Hudson,
James R. Antes, Erling O. Jorgensen
& Linda H. Hendrikson**

The transformative approach to mediation has become both a popular and a controversial way to conceptualize and practice mediation. While many practitioners are readily embracing this orientation, others are wary, skeptical, and even hostile to it. As mediators at a center that has adopted this orientation, we are interested in developing new training tools for our mediators. As a result of our experience in this area, we are hopeful that the classification and codification of opportunities for empowerment and recognition, along with specific examples taken from mediation transcripts, will help others to find utility in this perspective for their own mediation practice.

To place this typology in a larger context, we are following the path-breaking work of Robert A. Baruch Bush and Joseph P. Folger in *The Promise of Mediation*, written in 1994. In their conceptualization the role of the mediator involves identifying transformative opportunities, avoiding a purely problem-focused approach, and enacting a transformative response. Bush and Folger (1994) have defined successful meditation as occurring when the parties in the mediation process have been:

- made aware of the opportunities presented during the mediation for both empowerment and recognition;
- helped to clarify goals, options, and resources, and then to make informed, deliberate, and free choices regarding how to proceed at every decision point; and
- helped to give recognition wherever it was their decision to do so.

There may be more complexity in empowerment than implied or discussed by Bush and Folger. There is a vast literature on empowerment, much of it in the subfield of community psychology (see Rappaport, 1987; Roberts and Thorsheim, 1987; Zimmerman, 1995). Within the area of mediation, the

112

concept has been discussed in a variety of ways (see Cobb, 1993; Shailor, 1994; Kelly, 1995). However, for the purpose of the advancement of mediation training which is focused on transformative practices, we will limit the definition of empowerment to that provided by Bush and Folger (1994), "...parties are empowered in mediation when they grow calmer, clearer, more confident more organized, and more decisive - and thereby establish or regain a sense of strength and take control of their situation." They may be empowered relative to their goals, options, skills, resources or decision making. This empowerment can enhance the general abilities of an individual in other situations as well.

The process of training mediators to respond to conflict situations in ways that assist parties in taking advantage of opportunities for recognition and empowerment can be enhanced through the illumination of these concepts in actual and hypothetical settings. Transcript analysis is used here to illustrate situations where parties (one or both) may be creating an opening for the mediator to focus on statements and events that are part of the interaction between the parties that will enhance the opportunities for either empowerment or recognition, or both. Several of the transcripts were generated for research (Antes et al., 1996) in which volunteer mediators from a university-based Conflict Resolution Center (CRC) were asked to roleplay mediation for a study unrelated to this project. Others were taken from various roleplays created at the CRC. A final transcript, used extensively here, was created from a training video roleplay designed to develop transformative mediation practices. In all cases, permission was given by the mediators and roleplayers for use of the transcripts of their mediations.

A Taxonomy of Empowerment Opportunities

Review of these transcripts led to the development of two taxonomies of empowerment and recognition opportunities, which are presented in Tables 1 and 2. The opportunities in which the parties demonstrate **lack of empowerment** or recognition and **requests for empowerment** or recognition are provided. We have also given examples of **emerging empowerment** or recognition in which parties show indications of increased strength or perspective taking. Opportunities for empowerment are dealt with first.

As indicated in Table 1, a party's **lack of empowerment** can be observed and assessed by the language used during a mediation session. Statements that express confusion or uncertainty are often indicative of a lack of clarity. The party may be uncertain about what to do in regard to a conflictual situation, or may be expressing a lack of clarity about the problem itself. Expressions of anger, frustration, or repetitive statements may indicate

Table 1. Opportunities for Empowerment

Lack of Empowerment

Type of Response	*Illustrative Party Statements*
expressing doubt, confusion, uncertainty, or inability to comprehend	I'm just not sure that... I just don't understand...
inability to act	There's nothing I can do... I can't ... I don't see how...
anger/frustration	#!@&!
continued repetition of same point	As I said before... and I'll say again...

Requests for Empowerment

Type of Response	*Illustrative Party Statements*
exasperated questions	I don't see why....
seeking advice/suggestions	What do you think?
seeking change from other party	If only s/he would...

Emerging Empowerment

Type of Response	*Illustrative Party Statements*
shift from third-person to second-person pronouns (including body language)	s/he... to you... (turning to face other party)
shift to more specific language mean...	Let me tell you exactly what I
shift to "can" and "will" language	I guess we can... I could try...

a feeling of inadequacy toward resolving the situation that has brought the party to mediation. Repetitive statements may also reflect the party's own struggle to fully comprehend the situation, and may indicate her attempt to hear for herself what the other party is saying.

Statements that can be labeled **requests for empowerment** are also shown in Table 1, indicating the party's desire for empowerment. While seemingly only slightly different from statements which indicate a lack of empowerment, these requests signal that the party has achieved at least enough strength, clarity, or capacity to say that he/she wants more of the same. These requests for empowerment may take the form of questions, often asked in a tone which reflects the frustration disempowerment usually brings. A party may request help in understanding the situation or in finding a solution, sug gesting, if not a leap of strength, at least a tentative step toward greater empowerment.

Finally, this table displays statements that reflect **emerging empowerment**. This categorization reveals the fluid nature of empowerment as a growing state of clarity, capacity, and ability for decision making. The mediator might notice, for example, that queries a party may have previously framed very generally and perhaps addressed to the mediator, may now be reframed with greater specificity and asked directly of the other party. Even if somewhat uncertain, the party feeling emerging empowerment may begin to identify the nature of the problem with greater clarity, or begin to explore ideas for resolving aspects of the problem.

These aspects of empowerment, or lack of it, can be better understood with a series of interactions between parties and a mediator. The following transcript details a segment of a dispute between an older employee, Don, and his supervisor, Kris, who are working in a small but growing greeting card company. It clearly begins with an illustration of lack of empowerment, as seen in the following passage:

Kris: I'm getting a lot of pressure from my supervisors to, um, increase productivity and then they start taking a look at individual units. And they say, 'What about Don?'...And, um. I feel that I have treated you differently but I feel like I'm getting pushed and I'm at a point where I don't know, um, I don't know how much more I can do.

The supervisor feels like she has been ineffective so far in getting more and better work out of Don, and does not know what else to do to get Don to be more productive. She sees limited options, none of which is attractive to her. Another example provides an indication of lack of empowerment on the part of the employee:

Don: I really have some serious concerns about (confidentiality). You know that the reason I'm here is because of, you know, the bad report I got and some differences of opinion with Kris and I, ah, you know, is this just going to be another session where Kris goes back to the boss and tells him what I'm doing or what I feel or what I think, or, you know, I...I'm really concerned about this. I...I'm just not sure...it isn't really clear why we're here and is it just another inquisition to get some information on me that Kris could use in her quarterly report? I'm not sure.

This shows an overwhelming lack of empowerment. It demonstrates Don's anxiety, a sense of vulnerability, and a real concern about the purpose of the mediation. His fear is not only that Kris might tell the boss what he is doing, but report on everything he is thinking or feeling as well! It also leads to the perfect opening for the mediator to paraphrase Don's uncertainty and concern as he expressed it above about what Kris would do with the information gained through the mediation. Don then made the following requests for empowerment directly after the mediator's question was asked:

Mediator: How can that get cleared up for you, Don?

Don: Well, I...I guess I want to hear Kris tell me what she expects to do with it (the information gained through mediation).

Kris: ...it is a fact that your quarterly performance evaluation was not good. Um, and I was the one that recommended mediation as an option because, you know, to be really honest with you, um, administration was talking about putting you on probation and I really felt...that's not easy for me to tell you, but I want to be honest in this process. I do value you as a...as a person, and I also know from having worked with you that, that you really are a good employee, and I saw, um, mediation as, hopefully a step that we could take before we start getting too drastic...have to resort to a drastic measure.

Don: (asking for further clarification, now not speaking to the mediator, but asking directly of Kris) So what are you going to...what do you do with this information that comes out of this mediation? Is it going to become part of my quarterly report or anything like that?...Your evaluation of me?

Embedded in these requests for empowerment is also an indication that Don feels a greater level of empowerment than he had earlier - in other words, emerging empowerment. He began by saying he felt uncertain about being in mediation, went on to tell the mediator he wanted to hear from Kris, and then finally asked Kris a very direct question about how she would use information gleaned through mediation in his evaluation. We see the shift from third-person language to second-person language. The question was the same, but with the mediator's help he became more empowered so that he could ask the supervisor herself, directly.

How was the mediator able to assist in the empowering process? In this case, the mediator began with paraphrasing. Thus, after the initial statement above by Don about confidentiality, the mediator made the following restatement to amplify his lack of empowerment:

Mediator: So you're very concerned about what you say and how it's going to be used by Kris because she is your supervisor. You're real aware of that and up to this point it sounds like you're saying that there's been some dissatisfaction with what she's expressed with your performance and you're worried about it.

Don: Sure, and I guess that's why... that's why we're here. I guess, because of that, uh, quarterly evaluation and some other conflicts we've had, but what I'm not sure about is what happens to the information.

Here he repeats his concern and again expresses his lack of empowerment. The mediator then asks a question to find out from Don what can be done to address his lack of empowerment as to how that could be cleared up for him. As Don begins to address Kris directly the mediator remains intentionally silent so that Don can build on his emerging empowerment.

These examples show that when mediators are attuned to comments that reveal a lack of empowerment and amplify them by paraphrasing and asking questions related to them, parties are given an opportunity to deal directly with their own lack of empowerment. This sequence illustrates the way a party can move from lack of empowerment to a greater level of empowerment through an intervention in which the mediator offers a succinct observation, which is a summary of the party's identification of an issue. The mediator intervention allows the parties to focus attention directly on that issue itself. (For further discussion, see Jorgensen et al., this volume)

We have highlighted a number of points in the dialogue where empowerment can be developed. The careful mediator is constantly alert to the possibilities as they present themselves, and is ready to raise up those possibilities and turn them into the long-term process of assisting parties in becoming empowered. Over the course of the mediation, the parties may thus gain enough of a sense of their own abilities to deal with the issues that brought them to mediation. Further, with the renewed sense of self and one's ability, there is the potential to approach other life situations with a greater sense of personal strength.

A Taxonomy of Recognition Opportunities

The act of recognition flows from empowered parties; that is, in gaining a sense of self, a party may be more inclined to begin to consider the perspectives of the other party. A certain level of empowerment is necessary before a party is ready to give recognition. The mediator should be ready to highlight opportunities for recognition wherever they appear in the mediation process. Again, Bush and Folger (1994) have defined recognition by stating that: "parties achieve recognition in mediation when they voluntarily choose to become more open, attentive, sympathetic, and responsive to the situation of the other party, thereby expanding their perspective to include an appreciation for another's situation." A taxonomy of opportunities for recognition is presented in Table 2.

As indicated in Table 2, **statements that we would classify as requests for recognition are ways of saying "I want you to understand me."** A request for recognition may come as a direct statement in which the party may say s/he feels misunderstood. Emphatic or repetitive language may be used by the party to try to drive a point home to the other party. A party may make what sounds like attempts at face saving, offering explanations for behavior. Requests for recognition may include recitations of efforts the party has made or hardships endured that s/he feels have not been acknowledged by the other party. It should be clear from this discussion that, although Bush and Folger (1994) refer to recognition as the perspective-taking that a party accomplishes, the concept of requests for recognition refers to an expression of one's own point of view. Thus it represents an opportunity for one party to express how s/he wants to be seen and an opportunity for the other party to consider that perspective - to give recognition.

A party's **inability to give recognition** may also be evidenced in party statements. **Accusations, strong negative language, sarcasm, and epithets are clear indications of a party's inability to see another's viewpoint.** Words that indicate suspicion of the other's negative motives, or phrases that are used to trivialize or minimize the other are also clear indicators of the inability to give recognition. A less obvious, but often-seen indication of the inability to give recognition, is the offering of a spoken appreciation of the other's point of view followed by the use of the word "but," which is then followed by the party's own divergent point of view. The "but" in between the offering of appreciation and the other party's own view serves to make the offering a meaningless token.

Finally, **statements of emerging recognition indicate the party's movement toward greater understanding of the other party, or at least consideration that there may be another point of view.** In addition to the many non-verbal ways a party may indicate s/he is opening up to the other party, there may be verbalizations made which indicate that a new perspective is creeping in. Parties may actually acknowledge a new piece of information has been heard or comprehended for the first time. (Often these statements may be accompanied by a tone that suggests a request for recognition, in that the party wishes not to be held accountable for past actions committed without an awareness of a critical piece of information or an understanding of

Table 2. Opportunities for Recognition

Requests for Recognition

Type of Response	*Illustrative Party Statements*
justification/explanation of past conduct	The reason I did...
statement about feeling misunderstood	Nobody knows...that's not it at all
emphasis, exaggeration, and repetition	You always...
"here and now" language	Here I am with all this...now I have to...
how one wants to be seen by others	If only people would understand...

Inability to Give Recognition

Type of Response	*Illustrative Party Statements*
lip service, and "but..."	Yes...but
accusations, name calling, sarcasm	Ooh, that's original!
assuming worst motives of other party	As usual, you...
minimalizing or trivializing	Of course...she/he only wants to...
outright refusal	It just can't be done!

Emerging Recognition

Type of Response	*Illustrative Party Statements*
acknowledging a new piece of information	That's news to me...I never realized...
use of qualifiers	Maybe we could do that IF...
attributing better intentions	Now that I see that you...
acting more receptively toward other party	We can do it that way...
awareness of the other's points of view	I hear you... I'm beginning to understand why you saw it that way.

the other's point of view.) As an emerging recognition dawns, a party may actually say s/he hears or understands the other, and the absence of the "but," as noted in the inability to give recognition in Table 2, makes this perspective-taking appear genuine to the recipient.

In the interactions that took place in the greeting card company mediation mentioned earlier, several examples help us to understand how recognition can be given. We have taken examples that illustrate the lack of recognition, requests for recognition, and emerging recognition by the parties. The text below shows a request for recognition followed by the inability to give recognition, which is experienced by the older employee as he describes the history and dynamics of the situation that brought these parties to mediation.

Don: What happened was, Kris got promoted, and, as I say, she likes computers, she understands them, she picked up on that stuff right away. She became supervisor. Well, she and I worked. She came here very shortly after I did and we worked side by side and we always got along well. We didn't do things outside of work, but we always got along fine. And then when she became supervisor, that all changed, too. All of a sudden, she, uh, you know, was my boss. And...I don't know, just kind of pushing me all the time to do more and to talk to the customers less, and to get on the computer, and I...it's just more pressure than I can really take right now.

After this clear request for recognition, which also demonstrates an inability to give recognition, he goes on to express his feelings further:

And I really resent it. She doesn't seem to care anymore whether it's personal or impersonal. All she seems to be concerned about is, is how many orders we get out and how fast we do it. So I think it's kind of... the morale around here has really gone down hill because of this, not just because of Kris, but because of the two new systems we got. It's kind of stressful, and uh, I don't know. And then, my quarterly report, uh, was written up to say that I, I'm ... my number of contacts and my sales were way down.

In this passage the key indicator of Don's inability to give recognition comes in the sentence, "She doesn't seem to care anymore..." This applies not only to relationships with customers, but to the relationship that Don had previously had with Kris. She had acknowledged him as a coworker, and now he had been reduced to the role of an unsatisfactory employee, and he thinks that she doesn't even care about this interpersonal shift. He refuses to accept her presentation of self and sees her as an uncaring person.

The mediator attempts to summarize what Don had said and, noticing Kris' body language, invites comment from her in the following way:

Mediator: And Kris is kind of having a difficult time sitting and waiting. It's frustrating, but I wonder if I could just maybe summarize some of the things you've said. You've put a few things out on the table here, Don, um, that are quite interesting. It sounds like there have been a couple of significant changes in the workplace.

Don: I just want to say, you know, that I hope that this, what Kris said is true. That this isn't something now that you'll take back and tell everybody. That this is just confidential.

Kris: Don, you'll just have to trust me. I mean, I know that it's difficult, but I'm asking for you to trust me.

Don: Okay; excuse me.

Mediator: Are you comfortable with that answer or is that something you'd like to discuss further?

Don: No. I...I don't know. If she says it, then I believe her. She...she's an honest person. So I'll accept it.

This passage clearly illustrates a request from Kris for recognition by Don, after she has acknowledged that it may be difficult for him. The mediator notices reluctance on Don's part, acknowledges his discomfort, and provides him with some procedural options. When he decides he can trust Kris, he has had an opportunity to think it through in an interchange in which he was not subject to undue pressure to recognize and acknowledge his acceptance of Kris' commitment not to reveal what Don is saying.

As they continue, the following recognition from Kris begins to emerge, intertwined with requests for reciprocal recognition:

Kris: Well, you're right. It did get to the point where it was kind of difficult to sit and listen to, in particular, just the general negativity. And I think, to be honest, I think that's a lot of why we're here. Ah, you know I've told you before and I'll tell you again that, um, I really value you as a person. I mean we had a history together as far as I'm concerned. And, um, I agree. I thought we got along great. And, um, our relationship has changed. I mean, but that's just kind of the way it is. That's part of what happens and that's been difficult for me. I mean, I've missed the kind of relationship that we had, not just with you, but with our other co-workers as well. You know, I enjoyed hanging out by the water cooler and I'm sure that I do seem a little different, maybe even, aloof. But what's happened is that the things that I used to complain about with you, um, I'm seeing a different side to that. And I'm pretty surprised to see that there are some pretty good reasons for some of the decisions that are made.

For instance, the phone system. I mean, I know that that's been incredibly frustrating for you. Not just for you. I know other co-workers, people that have been there some time before we implemented the new system struggled with the transition as well. But, being in management now, I'm also aware that that's where we need to be to meet the competition. I mean, if we're going to keep our job, which is in everybody's best interest, we need to stay competitive. And, you know, I'm sure that you do miss the relationships that you built with customers, and you did have a following.

The supervisor took the opportunity highlighted by the mediator to offer the recognition that had been requested by Don. She is saying, in effect, "I recognize and empathize with you and with your co-workers as well; can you see the management position?" In other words, by providing recognition, she is asking for reciprocal recognition. That was indicated by the "but" she used to preface that sentence about her being in management now.

In the passage that follows, the role of the mediator in recognition is highlighted. The mediator is responsible for amplification of opportunities for recognition. This example shows an interaction where the mediator directly highlights an opportunity for recognition and amplifies that request.

Kris: Other employees have been frustrated by it, too. But for the most part, they've either gotten over it or accepted that that's the way it's going to be or they've moved on.

Kris first demonstrates an inability to give recognition by saying, in essence, 'You'll just have to get over your frustration; everybody else has done so.' The mediator takes that point, acknowledges it, and summarizes it as a key concern the supervisor has about the employee.

Mediator: You're saying, Kris, that it really does seem to be an issue of Don's unwillingness to buy into the system that's at issue here and that's what's particularly frustrating to you, it sounds like.

Here the mediator invites Kris to explain her perspective, so that Don may more readily hear and believe that the main issue is not his skill but his attitude.

Kris: Oh, absolutely!

Mediator: Say more about what it is that you would like Don to understand.

Kris: That it is never going to be the way it was. The computers are here to stay; the auto-dialer is here to stay. And I want you to be here to stay. You know, you really have been a valuable employee and you have excellent skills. And, I mean, you know, in some ways I kind of cringe when I hear you say things like occasionally talking customers out of buying something. You know, it's kind of like I want to say 'A-a-a-ah! I don't want to hear that!' But I know that's how you are. And I think that, um, I think that honesty is something that does retain customers. If you could just get over the negativity, your proficiency on the computer would improve greatly; I know you're capable.

Mediator: This is really a point of conflict for you, Kris, that you, you really do value Don.

Kris: Uh-hmm.

In this sequence, the mediator was able to identify Kris' concerns and provide clarity about them. More importantly, the mediator underscored the fact that the supervisor valued the employee, paving the way for emerging recognition, not only of Don's past performance, but also of his general business philosophy.

Hopefully, these specific examples can assist mediators in clarifying lack of recognition, requests for recognition, and the role of the mediator in amplifying the opportunities, which can be turned into responses that engender recognition. **As the sequences have progressed, movements can be seen which are bringing the parties closer and closer toward understanding. This mutual understanding can be the key element or catalyst for them to make decisions in their areas of concern.**

Obviously, there are many gray areas, areas of overlap, and shadings in these transcripts. It may appear confusing as to the category in which a statement falls. Lack of empowerment may be expressed as a request for empowerment, and emerging empowerment may be occurring simultaneously. An inability to give recognition may be tied up with requests for recognition or emerging recognition. It may be helpful for mediators to debate these kinds of distinctions with the goal of increasing their ability to recognize the concepts or categories. The important point is that mediators become alert to the many opportunities for empowerment and recognition and make appropriate responses that allow the parties to achieve clarity and address their concerns.

Taken together, empowerment and recognition can be seen as giving attention to the needs of both **self** (empowerment) and **other** (recognition). When this occurs within each of the parties, they have the capacity to improve their relationship beyond the confines of the mediation. They also have a capacity to create more meaningful and effective interactions with other people in other settings. **The mediation session(s) can be a microcosm or a kind of a sensitizing time-out in which, with a skilled and attentive mediator, parties develop a sense of working with other people in conflict situations in a way that ultimately addresses or achieves the promise of mediation.** This overall promise is encapsulated in the movement from weakness to strength and from self-absorption to greater openness toward others.

Beyond the Simplicity of Taxonomy: Guiding Generalizations

We have laid out the typology and provided examples of opportunities for empowerment and recognition from the transcripts of our mediations. These examples have illustrated requests for empowerment or recognition, lack of empowerment and inability to give recognition, and emerging empowerment and recognition. In the final section of this paper we will deal with what may be guiding principles for the finer points of identifying opportunities for empowerment and recognition.

If there is any overall generalization to be made about these opportunities, it is that they are full of complexities. In those complexities, however, we have found a kind of enlightened understanding, which leads us to feel even more comfortable with the concepts elaborated above and with the general importance of placing great emphasis on empowerment and recognition in mediation. The generalizations we have reached include the following ideas: (1) multiple opportunities may reside in single statements; (2) empowerment and recognition act in concert; (3) lack of empowerment is easily missed; (4) giving recognition is an intricate process; and, (5) receiving recognition is in the eye (and ear) of the beholder.

Multiple Opportunities May Reside in Single Statements: It's Fast and Furious Out There

The first observation we have made is that there may be multiple opportunities in single statements. For example, in expressing what appears on the surface to be a request for recognition, a party may well be simultaneously expressing a request for empowerment. An example of this can be seen in the following interaction between the supervisor and the older employee who was not performing at the level of expectation following the introduction of technological innovations in the workplace. The two had been co-workers and friends before the younger woman moved into her supervisory position.

The employee (Don) had acknowledged that he thinks they are in mediation because of the quarterly evaluation and some of the conflicts between them, but expressed uncertainty about what will happen to the information from the mediation process. The mediator has asked him how this can be cleared up and Don responds, "I guess I want to hear Kris (the supervisor) tell me what she expects to do with it," referring to the information from the mediation sessions. He has provided her an opportunity to give her perspective and by asking explicitly about this, even though indirectly, he is setting the stage for his own ability to recognize her perspectives. More importantly, he is clearly making a request for empowerment; that is, he wants to achieve greater clarity about the indirect results from this mediation. But at the same time, he is also showing lack of empowerment by talking to the mediator about what he wants from Kris, instead of addressing Kris directly. So, in this simple sentence lurk multiple opportunities.

The transformative mediator is aware of the multiple opportunities contained even in brief party statements, and makes ongoing judgments regarding whether and how each opportunity might be addressed. In the process of helping parties consider one opportunity - for example, by paraphrasing a particular statement, or asking a clarifying question - the moment will pass for addressing other opportunities. But because lack of empowerment and inability to give recognition are the fundamental experiences of people in conflict, "missed" opportunities will certainly surface again.

This suggests that opportunities are continually arising, sometimes in rapid succession. One can think of the mediation process as an ongoing set of opportunities. The mediator may imagine a fast-paced tennis match in which several balls are volleyed back and forth from one court to the other. The balls represent the opportunities for empowerment and recognition. The parties are in control of the game; the mediator is an observer, who in this particular analogy, has the ability to influence the path and speed of some of the balls.

Empowerment and Recognition Act in Concert: There is Harmony and Dissonance

It is easier to understand the concepts of empowerment and recognition when they are pulled apart and studied independently. Close scrutiny of each concept makes it easier to comprehend fully the complexities of each and how each is different from the other. The separation of the two, however, may cause us to fail to understand how closely the two are connected to one another, and how each one supports the other. The links between empowerment and recognition are powerful and important. They help to explain why conflict is so difficult (that's the bad thing) and to reveal the potential of conflict for creating an opportunity for individuals to grow in understanding of one another (that's the good thing). In our explanation of the links between empowerment and recognition, we will begin with a positive aspect of one of these links, and then show what is a negative aspect of another, related link. We will end by discussing one more link, which is both important and positive.

When parties begin to offer recognition, that is, to begin to really understand another's point of view, they become more empowered as well, because of the clarity that this new understanding brings. For example, in the mediation between the supervisor and supervisee referred to earlier in this chapter, Kris, the supervisor, is at first frustrated and confused about why Don won't put forth the effort of which she feels he's capable to do the work required of him. Don's failure to perform to the organization's standards has had a disempowering effect on Kris. She's struggling with him and doesn't know what she can do to "motivate" him to work harder to learn the new technology and service methodologies the company has adopted. This disempowerment, or weakness, turns her own focus inward, so that she uses their interactions as a time to defend her own notions of what she thinks he should do. If she could really "hear" Don, she would understand that the reason Don isn't putting forth the effort she desires is that he doesn't believe in the philosophy, which supports the new way of doing business.

Slowly, as their interaction progresses, she is able to listen better, to begin to hear his point of view. We would call this understanding and consideration of another's viewpoint recognition that Kris has offered to Don, but it's also inherently empowering to Kris, because some confusion is now cleared up for her. She finally "gets it" and realizes what's been making Don so resistant. This knowledge is very powerful for Kris, because it helps her to realize potential new avenues for dealing with the problem, which she would not have had, had she not understood what the problem was.

The example between Kris and Don supports a negative link between empowerment and recognition that helps to explain why Kris was so disempowered in the first place. Believing that one has already given recognition prevents one from offering more. We can examine Kris' viewpoint at the start of the mediation for an illustration. Kris has worked with Don for several years, and believes she knows him well. She, in fact, does know that he has a reputation for spending lots of time on the phone with clients calling to place orders. She knows that he has formed many long-term relationships with clients over the years. And she knows Don has worked for the company since its founding. She knows all of these facts about Don, but what she does not know is Don's motivation for the behavior she has seen demonstrated over the years. She may have substituted her own assumptions about what motivates Don to stay on the phone so long with customers and to have so many returning clients asking for him. (She might be thinking the customers fill a social need for belonging on Don's part). Whatever her assumptions are about him, they contribute to a feeling she has that she already understands Don's viewpoint—that she already has given him recognition.

This connection between empowerment and recognition is a common one in mediation, because parties often believe they already "know" each other. If, for example, Don had been a newer employee, or one Kris did not know as well, she might have realized she was unaware of his attitudes and competencies. She might have sought to learn more about him, and therefore been more open to understanding his point of view. However, when a party feels she already knows and understands the other, (is in fact able to give partial and credible recognition) and yet the other person doesn't do what is expected, that's a point of profound disempowerment for the first party.

In our example, Kris' lack of empowerment leads to the types of responses indicated in Table 1. She is unable to comprehend why Don won't just use his skills to do his work. She is angry and frustrated by his behavior, and is unable to find a way to make him do what she wants him to do. The irony here, and in many other conflict situations, is that while Kris believes

Don is getting in his own way of being successful, it is really Kris who gets in her own way. By believing one knows the other party and the situation so well, one may in fact be blocking the potential for offering the kind of real recognition, which would lead to true understanding of the other, and new insights into the situation.

This specific link between empowerment and recognition combined with a link mentioned earlier helps to explain why people in conflict have so much trouble. The clarity and understanding that come from offering recognition can be empowering; however, the offering of some recognition can block one from seeing the need to offer more, which causes disempowerment.

Finally, there is a critical piece of good news about the link between empowerment and recognition. **Feeling a little more empowered may make it possible for one to offer a glimmer of recognition.** Perhaps a party who feels an emerging sense of empowerment through a modicum of clarity about, at least, his own point of view can begin to consider that maybe he doesn't know everything about the other party and/or the situation in the way that he had assumed. To the extent that the other party receives it, this little bit of recognition that he offers may help her to feel more empowered, too. As noted by Bush and Folger (1994), one party's offer of recognition can be empowering to the other. Then, as the other party feels empowered by this offer of recognition, she, too, can begin to see that maybe there's another way to look at things, thus offering back a bit of recognition. These subtle steps, barely perceptible to the mediator, are the bricks in the path to empowerment and recognition, which can develop further into mutual understanding and genuine resolution of conflict.

In our mediation illustration, as Kris gained a bit of clarity and calmness (empowerment) through talking out her own viewpoint with mediators who were listening and paraphrasing, she began to understand her own thoughts better. This gave her at least a small sense of empowerment, which helped her to offer to Don more recognition than she had previously been able to do. **This incremental movement from disempowerment to empowerment, which can result in greater capacity for the giving of recognition, in spite of, or because of, the inherent connections between empowerment and recognition which make conflict so challenging, is what makes mediation work.**

Lack of Empowerment is Easily Missed: Weakness Masquerades as Strength, and "Power Over" is Not Empowerment

Bush and Folger (1994) identify conflict's potential as the opportunity for a party to move from a position of "relative weakness" (p. 85) and resultant "self absorption" (p. 89) to a state of greater strength and increased openness to the perspective of another. This great potential means that parties may have the opportunity to feel the heightened sense of personal capacity for understanding and responding to a situation that would allow them to take another party's point of view.

Understanding this about conflict is important for a mediator who is looking for opportunities for empowerment and recognition. It is therefore important for a mediator to be able to "see" what a lack of empowerment "looks like." But while a mediator can often clearly observe the unwillingness of parties to see each other's viewpoints (or can "see" the inability to give recognition), it may be more difficult for a mediator to observe what we would call lack of empowerment.

In Table 1 of this chapter it was noted that a lack of empowerment may cause parties in conflict to express doubt, confusion, and uncertainty. If a party in mediation conveys these feelings, it may well appear to all at the mediation table that this person is weak, and lacks empowerment. **However, weakness often masquerades as strength.** Table 1, in fact, also lists the following as indicators that a party lacks empowerment: anger and frustration, continued repetition of the same point, objections, and negative language. None of these attitudes or behaviors appears to the observer to be a sign of weakness. In fact, as many of our mediation trainees have noted, people in conflict often look and speak as though they are standing their ground and often appear to be very strong.

We need to look beneath the surface of this strong-looking behavior to understand its cause. It is when a party feels that she does not have the capacity to solve a problem or make a situation change that she is likely to become angry and aggressive toward the other party. **From a position of weakness, a party feels the need for self-protection and defensiveness, which are the fertile ground for aggressive and even hostile behavior.**

For example, in the mediation referred to earlier in this chapter between Kris, the supervisor and Don, the employee, Don can easily be seen as weak or disempowered. He shows the classic signs of confusion and inability to act that are easy to spot as manifestations of disempowerment. He doesn't understand why the way he used to do his work is now not good enough. He fears he will lose his job. He's afraid to reveal his feelings in front of Kris, his supervisor.

But Kris lacks empowerment, too, and it is reflected in her behavior toward Don prior to the mediation. Don describes Kris as unfriendly and impersonal toward him, and that she is continually badgering him at work: " . . . just kind of pushing me all the time to do more and talk less . . . It's just more pressure than I can really take right now. And I really resent it." Don doesn't see Kris as weak, and it would be easy for the mediator to miss it as well. She looks demanding and even threatening. But if we understand Kris' point of view, we can see how her aggressive behavior toward Don is the result of her feelings of weakness and vulnerability. As Kris speaks, she reveals the reason she is pressuring Don is that she believes Don is refusing to do work that he is perfectly capable of doing. This situation causes Kris to feel frustrated, ineffectual as his supervisor, and angry because of her own inability to make Don do what she wants him to do. This puts her, as the person responsible for achieving results for her unit, in a very vulnerable position with respect to her supervisors.

Speaking out of that weakness, she tells Don she believes he is "stuck in the negativity, and I mean . . . to be really honest with you, I want to say 'get over it'!" She's using some powerful language to describe what she wants Don to do because she's feeling incapable of making the situation change.

A second reason that lack of empowerment can be missed is due to the confusion many people have between empowerment of self and power over another. Again, back to the example of Don and Kris. As stated before, Don's lack of empowerment is evident. What's also evident is the fact that he is Kris' subordinate, which means there is a differential in their status in the workplace. Of course, we may realize that in a very real sense, Don has some measure of power over Kris, too, in that by refusing to do his work, he can indirectly jeopardize her status within the company.

But these status and situational factors are reflective of the various types of formal and informal power that Kris and Don may have relative to one another and not of either's sense of personal empowerment in this situation. Mediators are often aware of the various differences in power between parties in mediation, and can be tempted to try to balance the power between the parties. **Focusing on parties' power over one another, however, rather than parties' sense of self empowerment, will usually cause a mediator to miss the opportunities parties have to gain empowerment.** In fact, ironically, it can be disempowering to parties for the mediator to attempt to manipulate the power balance between the two parties, as it puts the mediator, rather than the parties, in the problem-solving seat.

Focusing on the parties will help mediators refrain from making their own attempts to deal with power between the two parties. This focus on parties will also help mediators to recognize the powerful-sounding language and behavior parties may resort to when they're feeling weak, so they will understand, and not misread, these important signs of disempowerment.

In Giving Recognition, All That Glitters is Not Gold and All That's Gold Does Not Glitter

Non-Genuine Recognition

It is common and natural for mediators to experience a feeling of satisfaction when parties demonstrate a new sense of understanding of the perspective of the other. Thus it is tempting to hear recognition being given in all statements expressing some discernment of the other's point of view. This is despite the claim by Bush and Folger (1994) that recognition can occur at different levels and may not be at all apparent at the table, either to the other party or the mediator. Consequently, what appears to be recognition, may not be after all.

For example, a party says, "I can see how it has been difficult for you, but I'm the one who has to deal with the customers on a daily basis." The opening phrase may be recognition; however the "but" that follows suggests that the opening phrase is an attempt by the speaker to invite the listener to give greater attention to the speaker's perspective - the phrase that follows the "but." Thus the speaker may be trying to make his/her own request for recognition more palatable. Or a party may say, "I'm sorry if my staff didn't consult with you before the decision...", and then go on to talk about solutions. It may be genuine recognition, but sometimes "sorry" is used with the intent to end further discussion of the past uncomfortable event or even to extract a substantive concession.

The point is that the speaker may use apparent recognition instrumentally as a device to further one's own interests. How can the mediator know? In short, the mediator cannot know because it is the party's motivation that is involved. But the mediator can (and should) note the context in which a statement is made. What has preceded the statement that may or may not give rise to recognition? We have two simple guidelines that apply to many situations. (1) If a statement is made early in mediation, prior to much evidence of empowerment, it probably is not recognition. (2) If a statement is followed by "but," the speaker has a point to make and is probably not genuinely taking the other's perspective.

What might be the consequences if a mediator incorrectly identifies a statement as genuine recognition when the speaker's intent is pursuit of self-interest? What could happen, for example, in the first illustration above, if the mediator paraphrases the statement prior to the "but" with, "So you have a new awareness now that the past few weeks have not been easy for (Party B)"? One possible consequence is frustration on the part of both parties. The speaker may be frustrated because the mediator did not highlight the request for recognition that followed the "but." The listener may be frustrated because the mediator has been misled by the other party. At the very least, then, a mediator responding to non-genuine recognition as if it were recognition will not be helpful to the parties. **A persistent pattern of misidentification could well lead to the parties' disengagement from the process.**

Subtle Recognition

It is important for mediators to remember that an implication of mediation from a transformative perspective is that decisions and discussions need not happen in front of the mediator. Parties consider information and points of view privately and after (or between) mediation sessions (Antes et al., 1999). **So, just because recognition is not overtly expressed at the mediation table does not mean that some perspective-taking has not happened (or will not happen).**

We have also observed that recognition might be expressed in ways that are more subtle than an explicit statement of "I see your point of view." It is difficult psychologically for people to move from a position of "I believe (X) about you" to "I was wrong about (X)." So they seek face-saving ways to express increased understanding of the other's point of view. For example, rather than specifically stating any new understanding of the other, a party may begin to consider suggestions made by the other. Or the party might offer a socially acceptable accounting of past misinterpretations - "That happened when our office was really short-staffed and the orders just kept piling up." What may be implied but left unstated is the explicit offer of recognition that 'things will be different now.'

In Receiving Recognition, It's in the Eye (and Ear) of the Beholder

Bush and Folger (1994) refer to recognition as increased understanding of the perspective of the other party. Recognition "given" by Party A to Party B (whether or not overtly expressed) increases Party A's clarity of the conflict and enhances Party A's relatedness to Party B. But there is also a benefit for recognition "received." To the extent that Party B perceives that Party A understands him/her, then Party B feels empowered.

We have observed that recognition, even when apparently genuinely given, is not always received. For example, a supervisor expressed a clear (and apparently genuine) apology for being insensitive to the needs of the supervisee. The supervisee behaved as though he did not hear the apology, and the supervisor continued to demonstrate understanding of the supervisee. It was only later in the mediation after the supervisee had the opportunity to express

131

his point of view fully that he began to show indicators of hearing the recognition being given. The supervisee was apparently so "weak" that he was not receptive. **The opportunity to talk about his concerns empowered him enough to hear what the supervisor was saying.**

Another circumstance in which recognition given may not be received is when the parties have a long history of strongly negative interactions. This leads the parties to interpret the other's behavior in a negative light. Expressions of understanding are received with suspicion, interpreted as non-genuine, and thought to be used manipulatively. Also because of a past history of negative interactions, parties may adopt a strict standard for what "counts" as recognition. For example, saying "I understand you better now" may mean nothing to a party unless accompanied by actions that also communicate the new understanding. The role of the mediator is to assist in the conveyance of the communication.

In this section of the chapter we have attempted to draw generalizations about the most important lessons learned based on our transcript analysis and our collective experience. Underlying each of these five generalizations is the critical importance that the mediator pay close attention to what the parties are saying and doing. The parties set the flow, the pace, and the agenda. This can be empowering to the parties and sets the stage for greater empowerment and recognition.

The overall significance of the typologies and these generalizations lies in the emphasis on the mediator as a facilitator of the communication process. Mediator attention is focused on the means that parties take to enhance that communication. As they come to empowerment and recognition through an active and satisfying communication process, the way will be paved for them to move toward a satisfactory conclusion on their own. Problem solving may then be a natural, but not forced, outcome of the overall interactive process.

ELEVEN

Microfocus in Mediation:

The What and How of Transformative Opportunities

By Erling O. Jorgensen, Janet Kelly Moen,
James R. Antes, Donna Turner Hudson
& Linda H. Hendrikson

The transformative approach to mediation is having a widespread influence in the field of dispute resolution. This approach was heralded by Robert A. Baruch Bush and Joseph P. Folger in their 1994 book, *The Promise of Mediation,* as well as through their continuing efforts to spell out the implications of mediator training utilizing a transformative perspective. Our own work in a university-based conflict resolution center has received new focus and vigor through engagement with their ideas and has resulted in our revamping our entire training model (Antes, Hudson, Jorgensen, & Moen, 1999).

Bush and Folger (1994) offered an important critique of the problem-solving approach to mediation. They challenged the directiveness that creeps into the well-intentioned efforts of many mediators. They were less clear, however, as to what specifically a transformative mediator is to do. Their general approach centers around the mediator helping the parties to capture the opportunities that arise in mediation sessions, opportunities for greater clarity and decision-making by the parties, which they called *empowerment*, and opportunities for one party to understand or appreciate the perspective of the other, which they termed *recognition*. Many of the "moves" (p. 140) they presented for capturing these opportunities were couched in the language of the mediator's speech acts and intentions - for instance, allowing, encouraging, helping. As trainers of new mediators, we have found it necessary to expand upon these ideas with concrete microskills that the mediator-in-training can utilize, even if s/he is not quite sure of the opportunity that is presenting itself.

In materials geared toward training, Folger (1996) has proposed three overall steps for implementing transformative practice. One is to *identify* transformative opportunities, two is to *avoid* a problem-focused approach, and three is to *enact* a transformative response. This general prescription, however, needs to be supplemented with very concrete suggestions for how to bring those desired goals about. Elsewhere in this volume (Moen, Hudson, Antes, Jorgensen, & Hendrikson, 2000) we have presented concrete indicators for the first of those steps, how to identify opportunities for empowerment and recognition. Bush and Folger (1994) themselves have detailed a persuasive treatment of the second step, why and how to avoid the problem-focused approach. In this chapter we will offer our sense of the third step, how to go about enacting a transformative response to the opportunities that are constantly arising in mediation sessions.

Mediators choosing to work from a transformative approach attend to moment-by-moment opportunities for empowerment and recognition. Empowerment refers to an increase in a party's clarity and capacity for informed decision-making. Recognition refers to a greater understanding by one of the parties of the other party's perspective, whether that recognition is overtly expressed or not. Opportunities present themselves in many ways (see Moen, et al., 2000), and are summarized briefly below. The examples listed in this section were drawn from transcripts generated for research into facework (Antes, Bryant, & Hendrikson, 1996), involving role-play disputes between two people who shared an apartment, one designated as the "Cat Lover" and the other as the "Allergic Roommate." In the scenario, the Cat Lover brings home a stray cat without consulting the Allergic Roommate to the apartment shared by the two and owned by Cat Lover's parents. Emphasis has been added in the quotations, to highlight the relevant indicators.

Indicators of Opportunities for Empowerment or Recognition

In our view, empowerment opportunities fall into three main categories: (a) statements which indicate a *lack* of perceived power, (b) statements which are direct or indirect *requests* for empowerment, and (c) statements which reflect *emerging* empowerment. A lack of perceived power may appear as confusion, uncertainty, objections, or use of negative language, as in the allergic roommate's statement, "I've been searching the papers to see what is out there, but **it's just too expensive** to move out." Requests for empowerment may appear as exasperated questions or seeking information, advice, or suggestions from either the mediator or the other party. The following comment seems to reflect an implicit request for empowerment by the cat lover: "I guess the only outward sign that I really noticed was that he was just sneezing... **He never really told me about his difficulty with studying** and stuff like that." Emerging empowerment may appear as assertive language, a shift from third- to second-person language, or first-person verbs such as "I can" or "I will." An example would be this statement by the allergic roommate: "I guess **what I want is** [for him to] put the cat in some kind of a cage or something like that when I'm at home... and maybe vacuum and try to clean up as best he can."

A similar threefold categorization can be used for recognition opportunities: (a) statements which indicate *inability* or unwillingness to see the other's perspective, functioning as a denial of recognition, (b) statements which are direct or indirect *requests* for recognition, and (c) statements which reflect an *emerging* offer of recognition to the other party. An inability or unwillingness to give recognition may appear as lip service, accusations, sarcasm, assuming the worst motives of the other party, or trivializing the other party's claims, as in the following comment by the cat lover: "He was all upset because he's allergic to cats and he was, like sneezing a bit,... **he wasn't really that sick,... I think he could live with it.**" Requests for recognition may appear as justifications of past conduct, statements about feeling misunderstood, repetition, emphatic language such as the use of "here" and "now," or statements about how one wishes to appear. This comment by the cat lover seems to be a request for recognition of his point of view: "It's just that, you know, **it kinda hurt my feelings** when he wanted to move out and he didn't tell me about it." Finally, emerging offers of recognition may appear as the use of qualifiers, attributing better intentions to the other party, acknowledging new pieces of information, or awareness of other points of view. The cat lover displays this kind of emerging recognition when he says, "I guess if I had known it was that bad I probably would have felt a bit different... I guess **if he says he gets swollen eyes and stuff it's a little more serious than I thought it was.**"

To sum up, indicators of opportunities to which mediators should be alert seem to come in three basic varieties - a stated denial or lack of either empowerment or recognition, a request for either empowerment or recognition, and an emerging expression of either empowerment or recognition. These become places where the mediator can slow the process down, and attend in a moment-by-moment fashion to the precise concerns being raised. How to enact a response with transformative potential for the parties will be explored in the next section.

Responding to Opportunities for Empowerment or Recognition

The responses available to mediators at such points as these involve a diverse set of microskills. Some of these skills, when used appropriately, are compatible with the transformative orientation and some are not. We believe they can usefully be categorized as three modes of response: *amplify, invite,* or *urge.* Thus, the mediator can a) amplify empowerment, b) invite empowerment, or c) urge empowerment. Using a similar threefold classification, the mediator can a) amplify recognition from one of the parties, b) invite recognition already given or being considered by one of them, or c) urge recognition. It should be obvious, given the values of the transformative orientation that the directing responses are not responses that a transformative mediator would likely make. We include the category here both because it helps clarify the invite and amplify responses and because it encompasses several skills that are in common use among mediators practicing from other orientations. Thus, it helps delineate differences between the transformative orientation and other approaches.

At first glance, the difference between inviting and amplifying responses may not seem evident. Certainly both involve responding to words or actions of the parties. However, there is a difference. Amplifying involves highlighting what has happened. There is no direct communicative expectation that either party respond to the mediator's amplification. It is perfectly acceptable within the norms of communication for the parties not to respond overtly. Inviting responses, on the other hand, provide some form of request for a response from the party. According to norms of human interaction, there is some expectation that the party will respond.

As mentioned, both inviting and amplifying responses are expressed in response to party activities. In contrast, urging responses by the mediator emerge from the mediator's ideas about what parties *should* think, say or do. Although the mediator's goal may be party empowerment or recognition, urging responses are attempts to orchestrate it, on the mediator's terms not the parties' terms.

At the end of this section, the modes of response together with the various microskills available will be summarized in Table 1. It must be emphasized, however, that transformative mediation is more than just a set of techniques. It grows out of an encompassing set of values, foremost among them being that the parties have what it takes to deal with their concerns. As expressed by Folger and Bush (1996), mediators "who successfully implement a transformative approach are consistently positive in their view of the disputants' fundamental competence, their ability to deal with their own situations on their own terms" (p. 269). The motives of the parties are also viewed positively by the mediator, who believes in the parties' essential good faith and decency (Folger & Bush, 1996). The modes of response elaborated below are ways to draw out and highlight the parties' own engagement with the issues of concern to them, whether for the sake of informed decision-making or voluntary perspective-taking.

In the sections that follow, numerous examples were drawn from a video prepared at our center for training in mediation from a transformative perspective - involving a role-play dispute over an employee's performance evaluation by his supervisor - and are used here with the consent of the mediators and participants. In the scenario, Don is a long-time telephone-order clerk for a company

136

that has purchased a new computer-based inventory system and a phone answering system that will no longer allow customers to ask for specific clerks. Kris, the supervisor, formerly worked as a clerk alongside Don.

Empowerment Modes and Microskills

Amplifying Empowerment

To amplify empowerment is to lift up something one of the parties has said so that parties have increased opportunity to give it greater consideration. **Paraphrases** and **summaries** serve this purpose. With a paraphrase, the mediator responds with his/her own words what the mediator understood the party to say. This is distinguished from parroting, in which the mediator uses the party's words to repeat what the mediator heard. One tendency we have noticed among mediators-in-training is the attempt to just paraphrase the common ground between the parties. This is not true paraphrasing, however, but **reframing**, in which the mediator attempts to direct the parties to think about something in a particular way. True transformative paraphrases, however, include the contentious material, realizing that that provides an accurate representation of a party's experience of the conflict that the parties have an opportunity to clarify and talk through in mediation. An example from the training video shows the mediator drawing out the basic philosophical differences that the employee has with his supervisor's way of doing business: "I heard you say, too, that the phone system is more troublesome to you, in a sense, that it really represents a different way of doing business that you don't like."

The above discussion focused on ways a mediator may reflect the content of the dispute in an effort to amplify opportunities for empowerment. There is also a potentially empowering effect when the mediator **reflects the feeling level** of the conversation. "It sounds like you're saying that the interactions you've had with Kris, even this discussion right now, have been very hurtful to you." Or, "You seem really angry." These kinds of statements are empowering because they communicate to the speaker that his/her experience has been understood—finally someone else knows how it feels.

A mediator may also amplify an empowerment opportunity with a **process observation**, in which the mediator simply describes what he or she is seeing in the process of the parties' interaction. For example, a mediator might observe, "You've spent the last 15 minutes or so talking about [topic X]. That was in response to questions you had about confidentiality." This is often followed by an open-ended process question, such as, "What would you like to do now?" or "What would you like to do with that discussion?" This type of comment helps parties clarify where they are in their interaction and the choices they have in proceeding.

Finally, a mediator may offer **meta-comments**, which are observations on the flow of the interaction, either at the content level, feeling level, or both. For example, the mediator might observe, "You began this discussion an hour ago with some strong statements about the negative performance review. You're not expressing those same concerns now. You seem to have set that discussion aside and have been talking recently about how you can improve your future working relationship." This is commonly followed by a check-out, "Is that correct?" The potential for empowerment is that parties can clarify what their thinking is in the conflict and be in a better position to make choices. But there is a clear danger here as well, a potential for disempowerment. The mediator is essentially saying, "This is what I see happening." If the mediator wants something to happen—an apology, an expression of support, a settlement—then those desires may influence how the mediator reports to the parties what he/she observes in the interaction. Such a biased statement by the mediator would have the effect of depriving parties of choices.

To qualify as amplifying empowerment we believe that such statements need to stay close to the parties' own verbal or non-verbal data, rather than importing and expressing the mediator's desires or point of view. The intent of amplifying empowerment is to help parties to feel validated and heard, to highlight their choice-making, and to help them focus and clarify their concerns. We believe it is a fundamental skill for transformative mediators, in that empowerment means to encourage the parties' deliberation and choice-making (Bush & Folger, 1994).

Inviting Empowerment

To invite empowerment is to encourage a party to say more about his/her situation and perhaps gain greater clarity about it, or to invite him/her to make a decision, whether big or little, about something that is of concern. It is one of the most useful ways for setting a transformative tone in a mediation session, in our experience. It is based on the realization that no one can truly empower someone else; rather, given the proper environment, people empower themselves. The transformative mediator can provide opportunities for that to happen through the frequent use of **check-outs, open-ended questions, and tracking questions**. For example, any comment or suggestion about the mediation process or what direction to go next should be followed with a check-out such as, "How does that sound?" or "Is that something you would like to do at this point?" Similarly, if questions about the content of the dispute are kept open-ended - usually beginning with "What..." or "How..." - that leaves maximum room for a party to respond (or not) as s/he sees fit. An example from the above-mentioned training video has the tone if not the exact form of an open-ended question, and constitutes a clear invitation from the mediator to the party who has spent the last few minutes simply listening: "I'm just wondering, Don, what is, what's going on for you at this point and if there are things you'd like to talk about?" Similarly, tracking questions request clarification or repetition of certain points in what has been said.

Requests to elaborate and **directives to elaborate** can also function to invite empowerment. These related skills foster expansion of a party's remarks, so that both the mediator and the other party can hear in more detail what is of concern to a party. Simple examples include, "I'm wondering if you could elaborate about...," and the more directive version, "Say more about that, if you would."

While a party is talking, the verbal or non-verbal back-channel responses—such as, "Uh huh," or "I see,"—can also invite greater elaboration. Traditionally these are called **minimal encouragers**, and are a minor way of inviting empowerment, along with the more focused **key-word encourager**, which simply repeats a word or phrase of significance to encourage the speaker to expand upon it [1] An example might be to restate the speaker's use of the word, " 'Upsetting,' you said." In the training video the mediator combined a very loaded key-word with a pointed directive, to invite greater elaboration and clarity from one of the parties: "Say more about what it is that you'd like Don to understand or what you'd like Don to 'get over'." This led to some very forthright comments from the supervisor, involving both empowerment of herself and recognition of the employee: "That it's just never going to be the way it was!... The computers are here to stay. The autodialer is here to stay. And I want you to be here to stay."

Urging Empowerment

To urge empowerment is to respond in such a way that the mediator's own data are part of the response. It is not only to raise up what the parties are doing, but to add one's own contribution to the evolving process. As such, it is not "following the parties around" in the directions they wish to go, but instead tends to violate a prime value of transformative mediation. It is nevertheless

---

1 In this sense a key-word encourager technically amplifies something already said by one of the parties. However, unless the party elaborates on it, the original meaning may remain unclear. For this reason, a key-word encourager is better classified as inviting further clarity and empowerment.

instructive to discuss some microskills intended to urge empowerment so that the reason their use is usually incompatible with the transformative approach may be clear. For instance, mediators are often taught to **reframe** comments by the parties that are too inflammatory, and give them either a positive or a neutral spin. The intent in reframing is often to move a mediation toward resolution, but by "sanitizing" what a party has said, the mediator deprives the parties of the opportunity to talk about what they came to mediation to discuss. Thus, this does not promote empowerment, but disempowerment. In a role-play transcript of a neighborhood dispute that involved a tree being cut down, the mediator attempted to soften Party A's statement to lessen the impact on Party B, but Party A wanted no part of it:

Party A: Well the contract didn't say anything, but he knew darn well it's my property!

Mediator: So you think he probably knew that the tree was yours?

Party A: I don't have any doubt that he knew it! And now he's lying about it!

Party A had the strength to rebuff the mediator's attempt to define the situation. There are undoubtedly many more circumstances in which mediator reframing is not challenged by parties, and its disempowering effect accumulates.

A frequent form of the mediator urging empowerment is that of making **suggestions**, either about the content of the dispute or, more commonly, about the process itself—such as who should go first or whether to caucus. Although suggestions are intended to be helpful and to provide needed guidance for the parties, they may have the opposite effect—depriving parties of choices they could make. For example, the first party to speak and tell his/her side of the story often frames the conflict in definitive ways, to which the other party must react. Consequently, even seemingly innocuous suggestions about who should speak next can result in disempowerment for one of the parties, rather than the presumed outcome of greater empowerment.

Other instances of urging empowerment would include making **interpretations, evaluations**, and statements of **self-disclosure**. Again, the danger is that these take the session in a direction the mediator believes would be beneficial but which is not shared by one or more of the parties. Thus, although the mediator's intent may be empowerment of parties, the effect may be just the opposite—orchestrating the dispute in mediator-defined directions takes choices away from parties.

We believe that urging empowerment is a practice commonly employed by mediators who claim that there is a clear distinction between content decisions (which belong to the parties) and process decisions (the mediator's expertise). But decisions about process always have content implications. Our discomfort with that approach to mediation arose from a sense that the stage model of mediation we previously used was too directive in moving linearly from one stage to the next, and thus ran the risk of being disempowering to the parties' choices (Antes, et al., 1999). For instance, after each party had a chance to share his/her own story, our common practice had been to strategize in preparation for the agenda-setting stage. The avowed purpose was for the mediators to decide a) what issues to include, b) what issues not to include, c) how to frame the issues, and d) what order to use in placing them on the agenda. We realize now, however, that every one of these tasks moves choices out of the parties' hands into the mediators', and so they are not conducive to empowerment. The transformative perspective reminded us that "strategizing" is a form of decision-making; therefore, it belongs to the parties.

Recognition Modes and Microskills

It is important to reiterate in this section that "recognition," as used by Bush and Folger (1994) and others involved in a transformative approach to mediation, includes any type of perspective-taking *by one of the parties* that shows greater understanding or openness to the other party's point of view. Thus, it does not refer to perspective-taking by the mediator. As presented above with regard to empowerment, there are three basic modes of response, which we characterize as amplifying, inviting, or urging.

Amplifying Recognition

To amplify recognition from one of the parties is similar in terms of the skills it taps to that of amplifying empowerment. It generally involves surfacing some instance of recognition—either already given or in the process of being considered—so that parties have ample opportunity to afford it full weight. This might take the form of a **paraphrase** such as one from the previously mentioned neighborhood dispute, "So you feel kind of sorry that you didn't consult with your neighbor when you cut the tree down?" It could be a paraphrase that clarifies some aspect of the past, such as, "So it was not your intent to..." It could also be some other type of **reflecting** back of the perspective-taking content of what has been said, perhaps via a **summary**.

Such summaries often have to **separate out double messages** so that both sides of an ambivalent response can be acknowledged. An example might be, "So you feel like you would like to change something but you feel incapable to do that at this point of time?" Here the desire to recognize the other party's claim is amplified by the mediator, even as the first party's perceived lack of power is also acknowledged. It is frequently the case that only the negative side of such double messages gets heard by the other party, so it can be helpful for the mediator to create a little space for even the small gestures of recognition to get noticed.

Sometimes, in the process of demonstrating an inability to give recognition, a party may imply that there are conditions under which recognition might be contemplated. For example, a party might say, "As things stand now, your proposal makes absolutely no sense!" With the opening phrase, the speaker may be implying that if some circumstances change, the other party's point of view could be considered. In such a situation the mediator might amplify this possibility with a statement that **clarifies obstacles to recognition.** For example, the mediator might say, "You don't like the proposal, but you also seem to be saying that it is within the current context that you don't like it." This could be followed by a question, "Would you like to expand upon that?"

Inviting Recognition

To invite recognition from one of the parties is to slow the process down (Folger, 1996) when there is an opportunity for one party to consider the other party's perspective more fully, and to respond in ways that give space for that to happen. Novices and mediation-trainees often think that means explicitly turning to the recognizing party and prompting them to reply. While such **prompting questions** as "Would you like to respond?" can sometimes lead to genuine recognition, it has been our experience that such overt face-threatening actions more often lead to denials of the very recognition they are trying to promote, or at least less acceptance of the authenticity of such forced responses. A related response is a **reflective question** such as, "Is there anything new in what you have heard?" The listener is invited specifically to reflect upon new understandings from the preceding conversation. This response is potentially face-threatening as well because it puts pressure on the listener to respond in the affirmative. **Circular questions**, in which the mediator asks Party B to restate Party A's perspective on the matter, also pose problems for two reasons: a) it is face-threatening to Party B if s/he was not listening closely, and b) there is a sizable risk of misstatement on Party B's part, so that whatever recognition there may be does not get heard or believed by the original speaker.

A less face-threatening technique for inviting recognition is to keep one's attention focused on that original speaker, and **paraphrase** what the speaker has said about how he/she would like to be viewed by the other party. For instance, "So you would really like (Party B) to know how stressful this has been for you." While indirect in its invitation to Party B (it could be placed both in the "amplifying" and "inviting" categories), such a response is more likely to facilitate a genuine consideration on his/her part of Party A's situation. Bush and Folger (1994) made an important distinction in speaking about recognition, that it includes not only the overt demonstrations of perspective-taking in words and actions, but also the more covert (or even invisible) events of "consideration of giving recognition,... desire for giving recognition,... [and] giving recognition in thought" (pp. 89-90). A useful watchword for mediation from a transformative perspective is that "small steps count" (Folger & Bush, 1996, p.275).

Urging Recognition

It is tempting for the mediator to try to make recognition happen. The mediator doesn't have the psychological investment in the conflict and therefore doesn't have the same barriers to seeing multiple perspectives on the conflict that the parties have. And since most mediators like to see parties reach some mutual understanding, the urge is almost irresistible for the mediator to share with the parties his/her perspective of the issues. When the mediator succumbs to this temptation, he/she is attempting, either boldly or more subtly, to direct recognition.

What is the harm? Isn't that one of the goals of the transformative mediator, to help the parties gain increased understanding of one another's perspective whenever possible? Stated most simply, recognition that is orchestrated is not recognition. To the extent that Party A's view of Party B is forced by the mediator, Party A does not genuinely understand Party B or the conflict. Nor does Party B believe that Party A understands him/her.

A tempting form of this mode of response is to simply **mutualize** and look for common ground. For example, the mediator might say, "It sounds like you're both saying that you'd like to be respected by the other," ignoring the different meanings the parties attach to the concept and different expectations they have for demonstrating respect. The mediator is attempting to direct the perceptions the parties have of each other and the conflict, attempting to create a false common ground, but this minimizes their distinctive concerns and thus makes genuine recognition *less* likely.

Some mediators attempt to **confront** or challenge the point of view of one or both of the parties in an effort to dissuade them from their own perspective. Not only does this have the disadvantage of distancing parties from genuine recognition, it also opens the mediator to charges of partiality.

A more subtle form of directing recognition occurs when the mediator attempts to go beyond expressing awareness or understanding of the parties' experiences to communicating that, from the mediator's perspective, that experience is "normal" or "to be expected." A common expression of this is

normalizing, in which the mediator might say, for example, "You seem to be very upset right now. That is a common experience for people when they talk about some uncomfortable issues or hear some negative things." The mediator makes a judgment about the party's experience ("it's normal") in addition to acknowledging it. Thus in saying that many other people have the same experience, the mediator is asking, albeit in a subtle way, that the other party also give credence to the first party's experience. In other words, the mediator is in effect saying, "This is how you ought to think about the first party." Similarly, well-intentioned attempts to **reassure** parties convey a judgment of the mediator that their experiences, since they are valued by the mediator, *ought* to be valued by the other party.

Urging recognition brings more of the mediator's data and perspective into the equation, and thus increases the mediator's influence on the direction of the conflict. The consequence is that parties may have diminished opportunity for genuine perspective-taking and thus less opportunity to understand each other and what the conflict is about.

Table 1 lists the various microskills discussed here, grouped by the mode of response used by the mediator—whether amplifying, inviting, or urging—and by whether they refer to empowerment opportunities or recognition opportunities. We do not generally recommend employing the responses associated with urging empowerment or recognition and that panel of the table is separated from the rest of the table to so indicate. Certain skills, such as paraphrasing, summarizing, or reflecting content, seem to apply to both empowerment and recognition. It should also be noted that different types of questions appear in different cells of the table. While some readers may differ with our categorization of a given skill, we view such disagreement as a healthy sign of engagement with these materials, in the attempt to apply them to one's own style and situation.

Discussion and Summary

In order to achieve greater understanding of empowerment and recognition and how mediator interventions can assist parties in the development of both, we have somewhat artificially separated the two concepts of empowerment and recognition, making them appear very distinct for purposes of clarity. However, it is very important to understand the dynamic relationship between empowerment and recognition. These are interrelated concepts that build upon one another. As empowerment emerges, recognition is more likely possible. And as recognition develops, greater clarity about the situation and empowerment toward decision-making emerge.

For instance, an earlier discussion in this chapter about inviting recogni-

Table 1. Mediator Microskills for Empowerment and Recognition Opportunities.

Urging Responses are Separated from the Others Because of Significant Difficulties Associated with their Use.

Mediator Response	Empowerment	Recognition
Amplifying	Paraphrases Summaries Reflecting Content Reflecting Feelings Parroting Process Observations Metacomments	Paraphrases Summaries Reflecting Content Separating Double Messages Clarifying the Denial of Recognition Paraphrasing a Request for Recognition
Inviting	Open-Ended Questions Check-Outs Tracking Questions Requests to Elaborate Directives to Elaborate Minimal Encouragers Key-Word Encouragers	Prompting Questions Reflective Questions Circular Questions Paraphrasing a Request for Recognition

Mediator Response	Empowerment	Recognition
Urging	Reframing Suggestions Interpretations Evaluations	Mutualizing Confrontation Normalizing Reassurance

tion suggests that a mediator who paraphrases to party A what A wants B to understand is inviting recognition from B. However this same paraphrase has the primary effect of amplifying an empowerment opportunity, in that A can become more clear of what s/he wants B to hear and comprehend. This clarity can create a level of empowerment that enables A to tell B directly what it is A wants B to know or understand. By the same token, taking another person's perspective can be empowering. It can be very freeing to finally understand what the problem is, and that understanding may only come when full recognition of the other's point of view occurs.

As Bush and Folger noted, however, usually the road to empowerment does not come through recognition. Rather it is the other way around - recognition often only comes after one is feeling clearer, stronger, more capable, and therefore less self protective. Strength and confidence about one's own perspective often allows for more openness and acknowledgment of the perspectives of others. It is this awareness of the need for empowerment before much recognition can occur that helps the mediator to an appreciation of two important principles: (1) despite many recognition opportunities, a party may not be ready to truly give it, and (2) acknowledgment and amplification of small steps toward empowerment provides the platform from which recognition and openness toward the other party may be built.

Another way to conceptualize the range of possible mediator responses is to represent each of the microskills along two dimensions, shown in Figure 1. One of the dimensions is the **extent of mediator interpretation** involved in the response and the other is the **extent to which the response enhances or interferes with the opportunity for empowerment and recognition.**

The interpretation dimension represents the level of understanding and analysis of the dynamics of the situation the mediator contributes by means of a given skill. It is obvious that responses such as **parroting** and **key-word encouragers**, for example, require little interpretation on the part of the mediator. On the other end of the interpretation dimension, such responses as **separating double messages** and **metacomments** require not only significant attention by the mediator to the flow of the interaction but a considerable level of interpretation of the interaction.

On the other dimension, the responses that are in the upper half of the figure - those that tend to enhance opportunities for empowerment and recognition - are generally those that reflect understanding, follow (rather than lead) the parties, surface the dynamics of the interaction, or encourage the parties to say more. For example, **paraphrasing** is a following response that demonstrates that the mediator understands the speaker, and often has the effect of encouraging the speaker to elaborate or expand his/her comments. Responses on the lower half of Figure 1 - those that tend to interfere with empowerment and recognition opportunities - limit the parties' choices, reflect judgment of the parties and their capabilities, or interject mediator input into the conversation. For example, **prompting questions** come from a mediator's decisions about what the party ought to consider, and therefore interject mediator input and may limit the parties' choices (even though this is not typically the mediator's intent).

It is, of course, true that this figure is an oversimplification. Our purpose in presenting this figure is to stimulate thinking on the part of mediators. The appropriate location of a particular mediator response on the two-dimensional layout can be argued, and appropriately so. For example, **open-ended questions** may vary in the degree of interpretation by the mediator. Thus the mediator may ask a party to say more about a topic just introduced (minimal interpretation) or a topic that is inferred from what the party introduces (more interpretation). Similarly **reflecting feelings** might occur following an explicit statement of emotion by a party (less interpreta-

Enhancing Opportunities for Empowerment and Recognition

Minimal Interpretation by Mediator

Check-Outs
Key-Word Encouragers
Minimal Encouragers
Requests to Elaborate

Parroting

Open-Ended Questions

Paraphrases

Tracking Questions
Reflecting Content

Directives to Elaborate
Normalizing

Paraphrasing a Request for Recognition

Reflecting Feelings
Summaries
Process Observations

Separating Double Messages

Clarifying Obstacles to Recognition

Metacomments

Maximal Interpretation by Mediator

Self-Disclosure

Reassurances

Confrontations

Interpretations

Reframing
Mutualizing

Suggestions

Evaluations

Prompting Questions

Interfering with Opportunities for Empowerment and Recognition

Figure 1

Mediator microskills expressed by degree of interpretation by the mediator and empowerment and recognition effect. Location of any mediator response may vary (see text). Responses below the horizontal axis are not recommended.

147

tion) or based upon more subtle cues in the interaction (more interpretation).

The appropriate location of mediator responses along the enhancing/interfering dimension may also vary. For example, a **process observation** that either does not reflect what is occurring at the moment or interrupts meaningful interactions between the parties may interfere with empowerment opportunities that are present, rather than enhance them as suggested by Figure 1. **Mutualizing** that truly reflects beliefs of the parties without glossing over or ignoring differences may enhance a recognition opportunity, rather than interfere with one as suggested by its current location in Figure 1.

As one moves along the interpretation dimension toward the maximal interpretation end, there is increased opportunity for the mediator to insert his/her biases. If the mediator does allow biases to influence his/her interpretations, the mediator assumes some ownership of the dispute and leads the parties in directions that may limit their choices and decisions. Thus a mediator may choose to **normalize** the emotion being expressed by a party because of the discomfort the mediator is experiencing in dealing with the feelings. This is in service of the mediator rather than the parties and moves the parties away from potential empowerment or recognition opportunities in dealing with the emotion. In a similar way, the mediator may choose to **reframe** party statements into specific issues for consideration. To the extent that this accurately reflects the flow of the interaction (in which case a better label might be summarizing, rather than reframing), this interpretation may enhance empowerment opportunities. To the extent that the identification of issues results from the mediator's comfort with particular types of issues (for example, substantive issues rather than relational issues), then the parties have been disempowered.

Thus, this figure should not be used as a fixed prescription for use of particular communication techniques. It is meant only to stimulate thinking by mediators regarding their degree of interpretation of party activities and potential empowerment and recognition effects. It would be a gross misuse of this figure to select a particular communication tool because of its location on the "enhancing" half of the figure and apply it regardless of the context. It is impossible to overemphasize the key advice in using any of these communication techniques, namely: *purpose drives practice*. If the purpose of the particular mediator intervention is to help parties take advantage of the current opportunities for empowerment and recognition, then the mediator has the proper focus. This point was elaborated by Antes and Saul (1999). They argued that deciding whether or not a mediator intervention is appropriate cannot be done without knowledge of the context in which the intervention occurs. For example, open ended questions are not always appropriate. If they are asked in response to the flow of the interaction, then they are used appropriately. But if they are asked to fill a gap in the mediator's understanding of the conflict, then their purpose is not compatible with the transformative orientation. In addition, Antes and Saul argued that the mediator practicing from a transformative perspective must respond to moment-by-moment empowerment or recognition opportunities in a way that not only enhances the possibility of empowerment or recognition, but also is compatible with other principles and premises of the transformative approach (such as respecting party choice and pace).

Conclusion

In this chapter we have attempted to link some common mediator skills to the practice of mediation from the transformative perspective. We have identified some mediator interventions that typically could not be appropriately used by a mediator practicing from this approach. We have also discussed conditions under which other interventions might be used appropriately. Figure 1 was introduced as a tool that mediators might use to consider if and how a particular response might be used in a way that is compatible with the transformative approach. We also introduced mediator responses (e.g., process observations and metacomments) that are not commonly listed as mediator interventions.

Finally, we offer the following specific advice for putting into practice the microskills we have discussed, with the caveat that it is not meant as a precise recipe and that mediation context and mediator *purpose* must always be considered. (1) In general, follow empowerment opportunities first—which is to say, listen for lack of, requests for, or emerging expressions of empowerment. (2) It is always appropriate to invite further elaboration, clarification, or decision-making. (3) It is also always appropriate to amplify whatever you are hearing, whether it is an empowerment opportunity or a recognition opportunity. (4) Be aware that the more interpretation you bring to a given response, the easier it is to take decision-making out of the parties' hands. (5) Realize that empowerment and recognition are dynamically linked and that they build upon one another, although not in a progressive, linear fashion. (6) There is a wide variety of microskills that can be used in any situation that have the potential of enhancing an opportunity for empowerment and recognition. And (7) opportunities that are "missed" by the mediator tend to surface again later, if they are sufficiently important to the party in question. So relax, attend to the parties, and enjoy the process.

PART III

Training within a Transformative Framework

TWELVE

Reflective Training:
Matching Educational Practice
with Transformative Intention

By Robert R. Stains, Jr., for the Public Conversations Project[1]

*The river down which we raft is made up of the same substance
as the great sea of our destination.* - David Whyte

I invite you to imagine that you are dreaming. In the dream, you are a conflict resolution professional with many years of experience under your belt. You arrive at a training about dispute resolution ready for something fresh. You're greeted at the door to the seminar room by a table stacked with training manuals and name-tags arranged in neat rows. You find your name, grab a notebook and enter, affixing your tag to your lapel. As you find a seat in one of the rows of chairs, you notice two well-dressed people at the front of the room. You think they must be the trainers, because they are busily arranging equipment, drawing on flip charts and talking with each other, their backs to the rest of the room. You look around for coffee. None in sight. The trainers look too busy to be interrupted, so you learn from another participant who is drinking coffee that she got it from a coin-op machine down the hall. Though you're tired and cranky, you find the machine and return, coffee in hand. People file in and find seats, murmuring perfunctory hellos to those with whom they make eye contact. At the appointed time the trainers turn, smiling, and begin their welcome. After saying how grateful they are that everyone has come, they talk about what they will be teaching you and what their schedule for you will be. They tell you about their qualifications to teach this material, which are impressive. They say they're hoping for a rich, inter-active experience and that you'll have a chance to get to know other

1 I am grateful for the input, thinking and practice of my colleagues at the Public Conversations Project: Carol Becker, Laura Chasin, Richard Chasin, Maggie Herzig, and Sallyann Roth, and for the reflections of fellow trainers of the US Postal Service's REDRESS™ Program.

participants by grouping up for lunch in an area restaurant of your choice. They begin the first part of their teaching with a 45 minute lecture.

Staying with the experience for a moment, what's on your mind right now? What hopes for the day did you enter with? What expectations are you forming about those hopes being fulfilled? How are these expectations likely to influence the level and course of your participation? What might the trainers do to shift your expectations? What are you thinking you might do to more completely realize your hopes?

OK. I now invite you to abandon the dream before it becomes nightmarish. This dreamscape could easily be dismissed if so many of its elements weren't common in trainings for conflict resolution practitioners (and if I hadn't set things up this way myself at times). This scenario fails to embody a fundamental principle of adult education and of a transformative approach: people want to be involved, and cared about. Many people, after experiencing this kind of "entry" into training, would find themselves less willing to take risks to advance their own learning, to "try on" new ideas or behaviors, and to express thinking that might deviate from the dominant themes being presented in the room. They might also be reluctant to share their own relevant experience, and less open to the influence of different paradigms and worldviews. Finally, they might expect the trainers to "teach at" them rather than collaborate with them to enhance their learning. As the tone of a training is being established, messages about the training are being received, attitudes are shifting and rhythms are being laid down that can be very difficult to alter later.

Just as most of us want to play an active role in the resolution of our own conflicts, we also want to shape our own learning and be recognized for what we already know. And we want to feel like we make a difference, regardless of the setting. These desires were recognized by the ancients: Socrates, for instance, who posed questions that called on listeners' own reasoning capacities, and Jewish sages like Hillel and Jesus who told stories that invited listeners' curiosity and presented opportunities to engage ideas at a personal level. More recently, thinkers like Knowles (1970) and Brookfield (1991) defined the bedrock of adult education as involvement: engaging the lived experience of the learner. Freire (1973) took the notion a step further, asserting the power of "dialogic learning" to shape social change. John Paul Lederach (1995) has applied this thinking directly to the preparation of conflict resolution practitioners with his "elicitive model" of training. Incorporating this line of thought into his own reflections on a lifetime of teaching, Parker Palmer (1998) has described the core task of the trainer: to engage the learner's "inner teacher" to act as primary agent of cognitive, emotional and relational growth.

Bush and Folger (1994) affirmed what most conflict resolution practitioners - and trainers - have discovered through years of practice: that people are more likely to be satisfied with a process and an outcome when they assume an active role in its unfolding. From the transformative perspective outlined in *The Promise of Mediation*, people are viewed as more likely to take action on their own behalf and engage meaningfully with others when they are in an environment that fosters "empowerment" and "recognition." Similarly, in a training context, a learning environment rich with empowerment and recognition provides fertile, stable ground that invites the "inner teacher" to show up and speak. **This chapter explores some ideas, structures and practices that are likely to result in trainees feeling empowered and recognized, thus becoming more available for exploration of the "new" and getting a "feel" in the process for what we hope they will support among their clients.**

The Transformative Practitioner

The ability to practice in a transformative manner springs from the heart of the practitioner. It rests on deeply-held beliefs about humanity, relationships, and conflict, and is expressed in the practitioner's capacity to "feel with" the parties, to discern their path toward empowerment and recognition, and to support their decision-making process out of faith in its efficacy. Practitioners must stand with the parties at innumerable crossroads of communication. They must see clearly enough to read the signposts for decision-making and perspective-taking opportunities and hold them up for the parties' consideration. They must be able to sense and reflect on their own emotional and behavioral responses to conflict in the room. Finally, and perhaps of greatest import, **practitioners must believe in what they are practicing**. In order to do that, they must have a felt sense of "what gets transformed" - and how - before they can make an informed choice to facilitate this process among people in conflict. **A training's effectiveness can therefore be measured by the extent to which it engages the prospective practitioner's heart, as well as her mind and body, in preparation for undertaking transformative work.**

How do we engage the heart of the conflict resolution practitioner? A training based on skill-set mastery and provision of "tools" is insufficient because it orients the learner toward intellect and behavior. Tools are ineffective if they are irrelevant to context. Tools can be dangerous when employed without understanding their proper use or without respect for their potential for injury. Tools serve well only when artfully matched with a sound orientation, a profound respect for context, and an informed sense of whether they will issue in results that are truly desired by the participants.

In the absence of understanding and a shift in values, appending skill-sets is ineffective at best and dangerous at worst. The successful transformative practitioner operates from a values base that forms and informs his ability to connect with parties to a conflict and to select the tools that will best surface the resources they bring to make their own decisions (empowerment) and to acknowledge the perspective of the "other" (recognition). The ability to think and practice this approach to conflict resolution grows from the person of the practitioner. **An effective learning environment provides a space where practitioners re-connect with their own transformative experiences, feel the effects of empowerment and recognition, and come to understand what they can do to encourage or inhibit those qualities in themselves and others.** The learning experience can then provide practitioners a much stronger, multi-dimensional, nuanced foundation that contributes to an informed choice of "tools" and skills, and to longer-term realization of transformative practice in their life and work.

Assumptions

How do we promote an emotional, as well as cognitive-behavioral, involvement in training? Before we can engage that question, we need to make explicit the assumptions that underlie what follows. The aim of these assumptions is to insure that the training of transformative practitioners is congruent with the **spirit** of transformative practice and that it provides opportunities for trainees to experience transformative **effects** while acknowledging that training **structure** will necessarily be different from practice "in the field."

- **Everything is connected.** Every aspect of a training can have real effects on the lives of trainees, trainers, and, eventually, clients.
- **"Attention must be paid."** Meaning will be made and conclusions drawn by participants about matters as small as coffee and as weighty as trainer-trainee relationships.
- **Experience grounds.** Practitioners are more effective if they first experience the effects of processes they intend to facilitate among disputants.
- **Better to respect than inspect.** An environment in which participants' knowledge, experience and person are respected and built upon is more likely to result in openness to new learning than a setting in which participants feel "inspected" for deficits that must be remedied.
- **Empowerment and recognition beget empowerment and recognition.** The more E & R there is in the room, the more E & R

there will be in the room, and the more E & R will be carried forward outside of the room.

- **Style counts.** Respect for participants involves addressing different learning styles by providing multiple means of engaging the material.
- **Transparency fosters empowerment.** Trainees are more likely to experience empowerment and recognition when trainers are transparent about intent and engage in collaborative processes than they are when an atmosphere of mystery and unilateral decision-making is maintained.
- **Relationships matter.** The "relational field" that characterizes a training can greatly enhance or detract from a learning experience.

The rest of this chapter will explore the implications of these assumptions for training design and the stance of the trainer.

Designing Training

A training can open our hearing to many inner voices. It can form the question that liberates the speaking of unrealized knowledge, the challenge that releases our untapped strength, or the listening that gives full voice to echoes of brilliance that have whispered at the edge of expression. When a training succeeds, it can inspire us to bring our most proficient selves to the service for which we are preparing. When done poorly, training can be a curse that calls up familiar voices of dread and defeat. Incorrect answers, mistakes made public through role-plays, and the comparison of our skills to the instructor's may leave us feeling diminished or incompetent in our ability to serve. **The charge to the trainer is weighty: fashion structures and facilitate processes that are safe enough to encourage risk yet open enough to welcome challenge; that make resources of both participants and trainers available.** These aims can be accomplished in part by setting a transformative tone and creating a "transformative field."

Setting a Transformative Tone

In both conflict resolution and in training, beginnings are critical. Cobb and Rifkin (1991) have researched the "problem of the first speaker": the discovery that a conversation's tenor, direction and content often are shaped by the first person to speak. Folger and Bush acknowledge the importance of beginnings as well. The first of their "Ten Hallmarks of a Transformative Approach to Practice" (1996, p. 266) is, "The opening statement says it all." In mediation, this refers to the mediator using her first words of the first face-to-face meeting with the parties to prepare them to participate in an informed way in a process that may be new to them.

Preparation of prospective trainees is also important. The manner and substance of the "opening statement" of a training can have a significant effect on how trainees enter the process. Participants are more likely to begin a training ready to try something new if they feel informed, valued, recognized and more in charge of their own learning. Setting a tone that leads to this kind of start is critical; it's very difficult to "call it back" if a process starts out on the wrong foot.

In the training context, preparation begins long before anyone arrives at a session. The "opening statement" extends from the first flyer through the initial in-class orientation by the trainers. From the time they first learn of the training, prospective trainees are making judgments about what they might expect from participating. Several pre-training activities can invite involvement, resource-sharing and openness to new approaches: printed announcements, confirmation mailings, pre-training interviews, arranging the environment.

- **Printed Announcements.** Announcements can give the first clues about how participants will be asked to be involved in a training. Effective announcements answer several questions: What are people being invited to participate in? In what manner are they being invited to participate? As receptors, actors, both? What kinds of shifts are expected to happen for the participants? What can they be expected to leave with? To contribute? What methods will be used to create a learning environment? The answers to these and other questions gives prospective participants the first clues about whether they are being invited to something fresh and new in content and process, or not.

- **Confirmation mailing.** A letter of confirmation can elaborate on the points hinted at in the announcement by going into more detail about training objectives, content and agenda. Care and interest in the trainee can be demonstrated by including questions for reflection that relate to the goals of the training as well as all necessary logistical details. Enclosing pre-training readings frees trainees from the need to depend solely on the "expert" trainer for transmission of content, allows time for interaction with the material, and invites the considered questions that result.

- **Pre-training interview.** A conversation between the trainer and trainee before the event accomplishes many things. When the trainer expresses genuine interest and demonstrates deep listening, the centrality of relationships to the training process is honored. When the trainer inquires about the background of the trainee and the resources he will be bringing to the session, recognition is offered and experienced. When learning goals and preferences are solicited, the trainee becomes a contributor to the shaping of the program and a more active agent of her own learning. When details of the process, content and participant make-up of the training are shared, the trainee is more informed and thus in a stronger position to decide how to participate in and use the training in a satisfying manner. Finally, when participants are given the opportunity to ask questions, potential misunderstandings and disappointments about objectives, processes and outcomes can be minimized. Individual interviews also benefit the entire group. By engaging in a deliberate conversation that has empowerment and recognition at its core, we increase the likelihood that participants will more easily know those qualities when they observe and experience them, and that they will more rapidly and readily offer them to one another during the course of the training. They are also more likely to enter the session fully committed to doing what is necessary to get the most out of the training.

- **Arranging the environment.** The ancient art of Feng Shui and the most current notions of architectural design operate from a shared belief in the power of the environment to affect how people think and feel about themselves and those around them. The quality of the training space is of great consequence: it is the first on-site cue that trainees take about how they will be treated. It can support or detract from training goals, lead to either feelings of eager anticipation or dread.

In planning the environment, we respond to the central question: What are we preparing people for? What is the journey we are asking people to take, and how can we support it with the physical environment? It's a similar question that a mediator asks when she decides whether she will sit between or across from disputants.

What do people initially see when coming into the training space, and what conclusions might they draw? I once attended a training where the first thing I saw was a small table bearing a pile of poorly-copied, stapled handouts and a coffeepot with a hand-lettered sign: "$.25 a cup." I began the training with a powerful impression of how much the sponsor valued my presence: not enough to kick in a quarter for my coffee. What the sponsor actually intended was unknown - and didn't matter.

If transformative mediation is about sensitivity to relationships, then the training environment should send clear signals that people are valued and that their connections to one another will be important to the evolution of the training. Small things such as artfully arranged fruit, flowers on the registration table, a handshake greeting from a trainer upon arrival, are as important in setting a tone as the more obvious examples of having adequate windows, break-out space, comfortable seating, professionally prepared training manuals and clearly-seen visuals. Easy availability of food and drinks - preferably in or near the training room, with a large space around the food table to encourage mingling - creates a social setting in which trainees feel valued and are more likely to connect with each other. A circular arrangement of chairs is more "democratic" than arranging people around rectangular tables. It also makes for easier sight lines and invites conversations among participants as well as between participant and trainer. If the tone has been set effectively, participants will already have experienced and demonstrated empowerment and recognition before the session formally begins, and will enter more fully prepared to be agents of their own learning.

Creating and Sustaining a Transformative Field

Once an empowering and recognizing tone has been set, the formal training environment can be structured - a "field" created - to deepen the tone, add to it, and encourage exploration of its implications for conflict resolution.

"Fields" can be thought of as structures of time, space and energy within which certain behaviors are more likely to manifest themselves than others. An iron filing caught between two magnets will behave differently than it would outside their pull. An unmown hayfield strewn with rocks will not likely attract people to play baseball in that space, or support the playing should they attempt it. A well-groomed diamond, however, would encourage the demonstration of those skills with clear baselines, level grass, room to run and a fenced boundary: a baseball "field." Margaret Wheatley (1994) speaks of the shaping power of the "field of vision": when the ground is prepared and maintained with a clear vision of what is possible to happen, the hoped-for behavior is more likely to occur in that space. What do we want to invite and support among people learning to do transformative work? What might a supportive field look and feel like? What are its contours, and how is it realized? After answering these questions with respect to a particular context, conscious use of educational structures and the person of the trainer can be employed to create the desired environment. The environment can be evaluated by the extent to which it enhances the understanding, experience and enactment of empowerment and recognition, as well as the performance of specific technical skills.

A training in a particular place with a particular group can be seen as a "living system" that comes together to accomplish a particular purpose. As Jantsch (1980), Peat (1988), Wheatley (1994), Benyus (1997) and others have noted, living systems will organize themselves in the most creative manner to achieve their purposes if there is **opportunity for change and self-reference within boundaries.**

Creating Learning Fields: Essential Elements

F. David Peat, physicist and biographer of David Bohm, describes "distinction" as a process necessary for the change and growth of healthy living systems (1988, p. 209). Wheatley (1994) discusses the need for an openness to the environment that is borne of freedom. She goes on to speak of the vital relationship of freedom to order, calling them "partners" (p. 95). In our work at the Public Conversations Project (Chasin, et. al., 1996) with people at odds over divisive social, moral and religious issues, we have found that **the sense of order that results from boundaries creates freedom and that opportunities for distinction create changes in perception of self and other: worthy aims of training.**

Boundaries in Training

Most people need some sense of security or safety in order to relax enough to allow their distinctiveness to emerge. When they learn that others value ("recognize") what they bring, they find it easier to entertain "the new," whether it's a new person, a different worldview, or an approach to conflict resolution that flies in the face of previous professional training. They also often become more interested in participating in a process of reflection on their own beliefs. Boundaries that support these processes can be constructed in training from the intersection of trainer objectives and trainee purposes, the planful use of space and time, and the collaborative creation of learning agreements (e.g., ground rules, such as allowing people to finish speaking, refraining from side conversations, etc.) that will best facilitate participants' realization of purpose. Boundaries open the possibility of experimenting with opportunities for change.

Creating Learning Fields: "Opportunity" Structures

Most readers are familiar with modes of instruction often used to train conflict resolution personnel such as lecture, discussion, demonstration and role-play. Tools are everywhere. Those structures can be transformed, however, by shifting **the way we think about** them as we create and employ them, rather than by concentrating solely on their specific mechanics. Educational structures become rich, nuanced, fully-dimensional and supportive of a transformative field to the degree that they honor the assumptions mentioned earlier and build in (at least) the following **opportunities** - each of which invites distinction - that may lead to shifts in perspective, feeling and behavior.

- **Asking.** The questioning process is powerful. The opportunity for trainees to ask sincere questions - of the trainer, of other participants, and, importantly, of themselves - allows trainees to feel more in charge of their learning. It can also demonstrate the power that inquiry has to shape perceptions and generate experience in the asker as well as the asked in conflict resolution and in relationships. The task of design is to honor the asking by giving it a defined place. A good example can be found in training designed for the US Postal Service (Bush, et. al, 1998) in which a full two hours is set aside for focus on participant questions.

- **Experimenting.** The chance to "try on" new ideas and behaviors in a safe-enough setting can allow trainees to expand their vision of the range of their capabilities. It can also enhance understanding of the experience of disputants who are invited to try on a new way of relating around their conflict. Experimentation adds energy and a creative "edge" to the field.

- **Personal Reflecting.** Experience and knowledge are much more likely to be carried forward beyond the training room if they have been engaged and examined in a personal manner within the training setting. Structures that support this process ask trainees to consider new learning in the light of previous experience; to notice effects on them of in-class experimentation with new behaviors; to assess the impact upon them of people in the room and the impact they might have had on others. Reflection as a practice can then be carried into the work setting as a means of insuring congruence between transformative intention and conflict resolution practice.

- **Proclaiming.** Trainees feel recognized when they are invited to declare their purposes, are given opportunities to share their resources and are asked to articulate their learnings and discuss their plans for application. As they are responded to by fellow trainees, they discover deeper value in what they have to offer and are more likely to seek out the same from their peers, valuing the group more and investing more in its quality.

- **Responding.** Planned opportunities for trainees to respond to sincere inquiries from trainers or participants provide opportunities for reflection, clarification of thought, and decision-making, among others.

162

Being in a "respondent" role also affords chances to experience the potential constructive or destructive effects of questions in the context of conflict resolution. The act of responding in a reflective mode can influence the tenor of questions subsequently asked, resulting in richer, less confrontational or competitive exchanges in the group.

When exercises, lectures, and other educational structures embed these opportunities into their intention and process, a field of curiosity, potency, experimentation and mutual valuing is invited and supported.

Maintaining the Learning Field: The Stance of the Trainer

The trainer remains a key figure after the structures have been designed, relationships have been created, and processes of change have been initiated. She is entrusted with primary responsibility for maintaining the integrity and purpose of the field that's been created and becomes the reflective presence that insures alignment of training process with the intentions of the transformative approach.

In the same way that the person of the mediator is critical to transformative mediation, the manner in which the trainer relates to others in the room is crucial to the creation and maintenance of a learning environment with transformative features. The trainer, for instance, may encounter expectations among participants similar to those encountered by the transformative practitioner of conflict resolution. She may be expected to be the "expert" with "all the answers" who will "tell us what to do." The manner in which she works with those expectations - and the people behind them - will be observed by participants for its degree of congruence with a transformative spirit.

Most of us have had learning experiences, which can truly be called "transformative": we experienced an inward shift, which allowed us to carry something new into our world. For many of us, these experiences were intimately related to the way in which a person in a teaching role (professor, coach, parent, mentor, trainer, etc.) behaved. I invite you to pause for a moment from your reading, and recall one of the especially fruitful learning experiences you've had with a teacher or mentor where you got even more than you imagined you might have. Travel in your imagination back to a scene from that experience and immerse yourself in it. Notice the details. What makes it so powerful for you? What shifts of mind or heart are you aware of experiencing? What is it about what the "teacher" does that enables those shifts to happen? What is it about how you respond that contributes? Based on this experience, what advice would you offer a trainer about how to be with trainees?

After doing this exercise with hundreds of people, some images of the transformative trainer or teacher have repeatedly emerged. Some of these images include: enthusiastic peer with a different skill and knowledge set; trustworthy keeper of agreed-upon structures and boundaries; honorer of "local"(i.e., participant-located) knowledge; facilitator of the realization of learning objectives; and catalyst of learning emerging from relationship.

Trainer as Maintainer of Boundaries

The trainer can be thought of as representing the group to itself, the mirror that reflects back collective decisions about goals, content, process, time: the agreed-upon boundaries. She serves the group, not by acting as "Border Patrol" searching for infractions, but rather as keen viewer that compares observations with agreements and presents discrepancies as opportunities for discussion, re-alignment or re-negotiation to better realize common purpose.

Trainer as Catalyst

In a chemical reaction, a catalyst is that element which, when added to others, enables them to create something entirely new when they interact. The manner in which the trainer relates to trainees, co-trainers and on-site support staff can be a catalytic element, a resource that can encourage people to "meet" in fresh ways to create new learnings. Through her behavior and attitude with others, the trainer furnishes evidence of the potential transformative impact of an approach guided by empowerment and recognition and provides signposts toward thinking and behaving transformatively with parties to a conflict. There are several areas where the stance of the trainer as revealed in his behavior are critical:

- **How the trainer uses language.** Important messages about the conflict resolution process are conveyed through the way it is described at micro and macro levels. For instance, when a trainer says, "What we're trying to get the disputants to do is...," a very directive view of the role of the mediator is conveyed. A different view is conveyed by saying, "The environment we're trying to create with the parties" or "the opportunities we're highlighting in this session." Language has implications for training relationships. The conscious use of language is especially critical when the trainer offers feedback to a participant in response to a statement or a demonstration of technique. Language grounded in an "appreciative" approach (Cooperider & Srivasta, 1987) highlights strengths as well as stretches. On the other hand, careless use of words, of tone and volume of voice can result in feelings of shame and embarrassment in trainees who have taken risks and impair the trustworthiness of the trainer in the eyes of all present.

164

- **How the trainer uses "air time."** While viewing a videotape of a very directive mediation, a trainee remarked, "The mediator talked more than the parties!," and commented on the mediator's control of the air space. Trainers can easily fall into the same trap through excessive lecturing, sharing of experience and "over-answering" participants' questions. A trainer operating from a transformative orientation starts from the premise that "the wisdom is in the room," and will not necessarily come most often from the trainer. This attitude liberates the trainer to verbally step aside and open air time to maintain a welcoming space for participant contributions.

- **How the trainer crafts and uses questions.** In a training, as in a mediation, questions are interventions. They are invitations to think along certain pathways that will conjure up certain experiences. They are also statements about the relationship of the asker to the asked. In a training context, questions can serve to reinforce old patterns of satisfying the instructor, exposing participants' weaknesses and creating a climate of competition ("Who can tell me what comes first, empowerment or recognition?"), or to facilitate a Socratic process of self-discovery and group learning ("Speaking from your experience, what have you noticed about the behavior of parties to a mediation that's led you to believe they were feeling stronger and more willing to give recognition?"). The transformative trainer uses questions to open new and creative ways of thinking about the mediation process rather than to test trainees' knowledge or retention of classroom material.

- **How the trainer answers questions.** The temptation for the trainer to adopt the "expert stance" is at its height when a question is asked. Even trainers with the best of intentions, especially those with a great deal of experience in the subject area, can get seduced by a question that seems to invite them to lay out the full range of their experience and knowledge on a particular point. This "over-answering" can easily result in participants shifting their perception of the trainer to a more "elevated" or distant stance while devaluing their own experience. Responding briefly and then "checking-in" with the questioner is a more respectful practice.

- **How the trainer frames exercises.** The functions of an exercise in the transformative orientation are, among others, to help trainees discover and articulate the knowledge they possess and to extend it through exposure to the knowledge and experience of others, both participants and trainer. Exercises can be posed in a way that invites this manner of learning to occur ("We'll ask you to notice how this style of questioning affects you, and what some of the implications might be for using this style in a mediation"), or in a manner that prepares the trainee to be "worked upon" by some external force which will also impart knowledge in the process ("In this exercise we will show you that...").

- **How the trainer uses his/her body.** Where the trainer places his body has an impact on whether communication is promoted among participants or between individual trainees and the trainer. For instance, sitting in a circle with trainees can have a communitarian or democratizing effect, while sitting at the head of a long table tends to push the flow of conversation toward the trainer. Likewise, some trainers like to remain standing and move toward trainees when they are responding to a question or offering an observation. This can have the negative effect of creating a staccato series of dyadic interchanges with the trainer rather than a cybernetic flow of communication among participants. If the trainer sits down when trainees respond at length or pulls his/her chair back from the circle a bit, information and energy is more easily shared by the entire group and communications can build on one another.

- **How the trainer interacts with a co-trainer.** In post-training evaluations, many participants have reported that a powerful part of a learning experience has been to watch the way trainers have behaved with one another. Learnings will be taken from their interactions that either support or de-legitimize what is being taught about relationship. The fabric of the co-trainer relationship which is most congruent with a transformative approach is woven through with threads of recognition and empowerment: mutual respect is granted when difference arises; each is secure enough in his or her own strength that each celebrates the strength of the other. This is not an easy task. Co-training is "relationship under the lights." There are high levels of expectation, important tasks to be done, and anxiety filling the air. What might be minor relational glitches in another setting suddenly feel immense. When approached with forethought and a sense of humor, however, a well-functioning relationship can anchor the abstract concepts with a living, breathing example of what is possible. Advanced planning of the relational elements of a co-training relationship is critical. This means getting together not just to divvy up the agenda, but also to candidly discuss what each person needs and wants from the other, how each wishes to receive feedback about mistakes, how to include trainer differences without ruining the flow, etc.

- **How the trainer relates with on-site support staff.** Right or wrong, many trainees want to know if we really believe what we teach or if it's just an act that's grown out of the latest educational fad. Trainees are rightly suspicious of the integrity of a trainer's commitment to transformative values when they see him behaving in a different manner toward support staff (A/V technicians, interns, maintenance people, etc.) than he does with trainees or co-trainers. Trainers are presented with repeated opportunities to "walk the talk."

Conclusion

Creating an environment that invites empowerment and recognition is as important to the training of practitioners of a transformative approach as it is to parties who want to work through conflicts constructively. Assuring the congruence of training process with transformative intent is an ongoing part of the training mission. It may be achieved by setting a transformative tone, designing and maintaining a transformative field, and attending to and reflecting on the stance and role of the trainer.

THIRTEEN

Developing Transformative Training:
A View From the Inside

By Joseph P. Folger & Robert A. Baruch Bush

It is often said that "those who can't do, teach." As two long-term university professors who worry about the perils of being "academics," we have taken this adage as a clear warning. We have tried through the years not to allow our teaching responsibilities and university commitments to divert our practice skills. Instead, we have tried to balance our interest in conflict and alternative dispute resolution theory with sustained practical experience in the field. We have remained committed to being "hands on" as well as "heads on" as we developed ideas about conflict and mediation practice. Although keeping this balance proves difficult at times, we constantly strive for it because we firmly believe that most insightful learning comes from doing.

In writing *The Promise of Mediation* we relied heavily on the mediations we conducted through the Hofstra University Mediation Clinic to develop the central ideas about a transformative approach to practice. Since the publication of this book, we have relied on our experience in developing trainings for beginning and advanced mediators to obtain greater clarity about how to convey the transformative approach and how to assist people who are attempting to master it for themselves in their own arenas of practice.

This chapter draws on our experience in developing and delivering these trainings. We summarize several key training themes that emerged as we designed and reflected upon the mediation trainings we have conducted. **These themes capture some of the explicit and implicit premises that guide our thinking about how to develop new methods for teaching mediation practice skills, in light of the transformative framework.** These training themes are best thought of as guideposts that trainers can use to shape the development of more specific training elements (exercises, mini-lectures, role plays, etc.) Many of these themes provide a key link between purpose and practice — they tie the underlying theory that drives mediators' sense of purpose to specific mediation practice techniques that have been developed for training. In this sense, they are "meta-theories" of training that can be drawn upon to develop new approaches to training within the transformative framework.

Be Transparent About the "Purpose of Practice"

An important goal of either a basic or advanced training should be to encourage mediators to think through the underlying assumptions they bring to their practice. Many trainings in the mediation field are designed around models of the mediation process (e.g., the stages of a mediation session) and specific third party skills (e.g., conducting opening statements or caucuses, paraphrasing, listening). Rarely, however, do existing mediation trainings thoroughly examine the underlying assumptions on which the set of training elements are based. Stages of the process and specific skills employed during the process rest on implicit assumptions about what productive conflict interaction is. These assumptions shape models of the process and guide mediators in their use of third-party skills. Training formats often overlook the fact that any practice skill can lead to very different ends and create very different forms of intervention depending on how mediators conceive of their purpose — how they use the specific skill they have been taught. As a result, it is crucial that trainings developed within the transformative framework encourage trainees to examine the goals and values that mediation can serve (or disserve). **Examining these premises provides mediators with a clear sense of how their assumptions about the goals of the process steer their decisions about what to do at any moment during a session.** It illustrates the way purpose drives practice.

In the transformative framework, the purpose of mediation practice is tied to a relational worldview and a transformative vision of conflict and conflict intervention. Understanding the premises of practice therefore involves exploring the assumptions about human nature and the nature of conflict that flow from this relational vision in the training itself. These "theory" discussions have taken different forms in different trainings, but all have asked trainees to consider the following:

- the meaning of a relational worldview - what it means to remain committed to a view that people are capable of compassionate strength;
- the view that conflict is productive when people move from states of weakness to strength, and from states of self-absorption to openness to others;
- the view that conflict intervention primarily involves working with opportunities for empowerment and recognition;
- the possible outcomes of an approach to mediation that is centered on the parties' conflict interaction, and its transformation.

These issues have been approached from many different directions in various trainings. The approach to covering these issues is largely one of the trainer's preference and his or her own instincts about what works best with beginning or advanced mediators. For example, the material on the premises of practice works best for some trainers at the very beginning of a seminar because the theoretical orientation provides a solid foundation for all practice skills introduced at a later point in the training. It clarifies how purpose drives practice before any skill is demonstrated. Other trainers include the theory section later in the training, after trainees have been immersed in some of the practice skills and have a more vivid sense of what practice looks like within the transformative framework. In this case, the examples provide an experiential base from which to understand the way purpose drives practice.

A second choice in conducting discussions of underlying premises centers around the issue of whether the trainer should provide a comparison of ideological premises. Should the theory section compare, for example, individualistic/settlement-oriented practice and relational/transformative practice? Or should only the transformative framework be presented? This is a more difficult decision than might appear at first glance. Comparing premises is often a good way to clarify the goals of transformative practice — people often learn best by thinking clearly about what is outside the realm of transformative mediation. But the comparison may actually seem to some of the trainees to be a digression from the goals of the training itself. When we have conducted training sessions for beginning mediators and compared frameworks, the comparison seemed to take the training off track, leading trainees to wonder if the comparison was aimed more at a discussion of "politics in the field" than for actually helping them to learn how to practice. For advanced mediation trainings where trainees are familiar with a settlement-oriented form of practice, the comparison often helps bring home the difference in goals. But it also sometimes leads to an emotional debate during the training about the value of each approach. People who have practiced from an alternative approach may feel threatened by the comparison, even if this comparison is done in a non-judgmental manner. If the transformative model is going to be taught in the training, the trainees recognize – as they naturally would – that the trainer has made a choice, a preference for practice. The aura of judging the models is inescapable. This discussion may or may not assist in reaching the instructional goals of the training itself. It is often helpful, though, in encouraging experienced mediators to think through for themselves how they want to practice and what commitments their choice entails.

Illustrate a Proactive, Non-directive Role for Mediators

In introducing the transformative framework there is a tendency for trainees to believe that the way to avoid directiveness is for mediators to remain passive. This is especially true for mediators who have been taught alternative approaches to practice that explicitly or implicitly encourage mediators to feel responsible for achieving settlement and thus promote substantial influence over the development of the parties' issues. When mediators have practiced within this approach, it is often difficult for them to envision the proactive role mediators adopt when they are attempting to work within a transformative approach. **In terms of training design, this means that trainers need to place strong emphasis on illustrating the way in which mediators can actively follow, rather than lead parties — that is, on describing the role for a mediator whose aim is to focus on processes of empowerment and recognition.**

The strategies for accomplishing this goal in training center primarily on instructing mediators how to sustain a "micro-focus" throughout a mediation session. **This approach instructs mediators to focus on the moment-to-moment interaction that is constantly unfolding — on the specific individual comments and responses that parties are making.** Sustaining this focus allows mediators to work with the conflict interaction as it unfolds, without jumping ahead to possible endpoints or outcomes of the dispute as a whole. For example, a micro-focus diverts mediators from the tendency to hear parties' opening "stories" as the representation of the conflict issues and to quickly shape those stories into some global conception of a problem that can be solved. This macro-focus moves the mediator's attention beyond the here and now of the interaction in the room. It can easily lead to substantial influence over the direction the conflict takes because it begins to limit where the parties can go with their conflict interaction during the rest of the mediation. It sets an agenda that can stand in the way of allowing the parties to address what they want to address. It diverts attention away from letting the focus of the intervention be on changes in the parties' own conflict interaction.

Instead, the micro-focus keeps the mediator's attention on the specific opportunities for empowerment and recognition that are revealed comment-by-comment during a mediation session. The goal for the mediator is to stay in the moment as much as possible and to allow this focus to create the outcomes that the parties want to achieve. It is through this approach that mediators learn how to follow parties rather than lead them and that allows for the possible transformation of the parties' conflict interaction, not just the settlement of specific issues.

Teaching mediators how to sustain a micro-focus requires the use of training techniques that can best illustrate the moment-to-moment choices that are made as a mediation unfolds. One way to accomplish this is to rely on "critical point" role plays that enable both trainer and trainee to focus on specific moments of interaction during the process. Critical point role plays are designed around short scenes that focus attention on one statement that a party has made at some key point during a session. In working with the critical point, trainees are asked to 1) identify the opportunity for empowerment and/or recognition that the parties' statement reveals 2) suggest or actually role play the next statement that the mediator could make in response to the party's comment. Critical point role plays can also be done in sequence by running through a continuous role play of a mediation session but breaking the session into very short 5-10 minute segments. Each segment is discussed before proceeding to the next, clarifying the opportunities for empowerment and recognition that arose and were responded to during the interaction segment. These mini role plays keep trainees' attention on only one comment at a time in the context of what has just happened during the session, thereby clarifying and reinforcing what it means to adopt a micro-focus mindset.

Critical point roles plays are innovative approaches to training, consistent with the non-directive character of transformative practice. They stand in contrast to standard approaches to role-playing used in many mediation trainings, where the emphasis is on illustrating broader phases of a mediation session, or even an entire session, and providing feedback at the end. These longer role plays do not serve the instructional goals of a transformative training because they do not instruct mediators on how to hear the opportunities for empowerment and recognition in the individual comments parties make and they encourage mediators to think more globally about the what the dispute as a whole is about, rather than on the conflict interaction as it unfolds. Training activities that teach mediators how to micro-focus are crucial in developing skills that prevent more directive forms of practice.

Provide a Big-Picture Contrast of Problem-Solving and Transformative Practice

In addition to including training techniques that provide skill in micro-focusing, we have found it useful in training to illustrate the overall difference between a problem-solving approach and a transformative orientation. Providing the "big picture" difference between these forms of practice is important for several reasons.

First, trainees need to see the way an entire mediation session, or a significant portion of one, progresses to be able to see the cyclical, non-linear character of an intervention that is based in processes of empowerment and recognition. It is only by seeing a longer, or more complete intervention that trainees can obtain a realistic sense of the patterns, cycles and eventual movement in parties' interaction, and can contrast this with the more controlled, linear and phasic character of problem-solving sessions. In seeing a transformative intervention, trainees recognize patterns of interaction that occur naturally as conflict begins to head in more productive directions.

Second, **it is by watching longer segments of a mediation session that trainees come to see how empowerment and recognition are interdependent, building on each other incrementally and cumulatively during a session.** Depictions of longer segments of a mediation convey how groundwork set early in a session can support, at a later point, parties' clarity about the choices they want to make or their ability to acknowledge or recognize each other. In many conflicts, for example, parties need to move towards a greater sense of clarity about what their concerns, resources, choices etc. are before they can begin to open up to the other's point of view. Watching this happen over time in a mediation session allows trainees to see that recognition may happen naturally at a later point in the session and should not be forced by the mediator. It also clarifies some of the choices mediators might make in working with opportunities for party empowerment at the outset of a session thereby laying the groundwork for recognition. This connection between party empowerment and inter-party recognition can only be seen by observing longer segments of mediation sessions.

Finally, seeing complete (or nearly complete) mediation sessions that compare problem-solving and transformative mediation enables trainees to assess the impact of the mediation as a whole. They can begin to gain a sense of whether the interaction among the parties has been changed and, if so, how it has shifted. Trainers can conduct instructive discussions about what new understandings the parties developed of themselves or each other, what the parties' interaction might look like after the session, or how the parties might realistically deal with future conflicts as a direct result of the changes in their conflict interaction. Discussions of these outcomes put mediators in touch with the potential "upstream effects" of a transformative approach to practice - how mediation can impact parties' interaction in ways that continue after the session and can influence the organizational, family or community settings in which the parties live.

To convey these big-picture differences, we have relied primarily on videos of mediation sessions we have created. We created "mock-up" videos based on existing training tapes currently used in standard trainings to depict realistic problem-solving mediation. That is, the facts and context used on an existing training tape were changed, but the role player who played the mediator on the new tape employed similar intervention techniques and made similar moves throughout the session. This approach allowed us to depict realistic, non-caricatured examples of problem-solving practice. In some advanced mediation trainings, we have shown fairly long video segments (one half hour or more) of different mediators interacting with the same parties over the same issues. The first two mediators illustrated highly directive and subtly directive problem-solving mediation. The third mediator illustrated a transformative approach to the same case.

There are many insights that come from showing these contrasting mediation sessions. Watching the videos helps people honestly assess their current approach to practice. It is easy to believe, in principle, that one is committed to a transformative framework, but prior training and the pressures that arise during an actual session often lead to substantial directiveness without much conscious awareness. In watching the contrasting videotapes we have created, practicing mediators often "see themselves" in the mediators who are enacting either the strongly or subtly directive forms of problem-solving practice. They begin to recognize how certain forms of practice are actually quite directive, even though when they are engaged in them, they may seem to be quite innocuous or even "helpful."

These contrasting videos also allow trainees to observe both verbal and nonverbal behaviors that are consistent or inconsistent with a transformative approach to practice. The video demonstrations of transformative practice illustrate the way in which the mediator continuously sends cues that indicate he/she is clearly following the parties' lead on where they want to go with their conflict interaction. Trainees see, for example, the way a mediator can continuously "check in" with the parties to see if they want to speak or where they want to focus their discussion at any given moment. This "checking in" behavior stands in sharp contrast to the behavior of mediators on the problem-solving videos. In these sessions, the mediators are setting agendas, marking boundaries for how issues will be discussed and ignoring or avoiding cues from the parties that could signal they are uncomfortable with the direction the interaction is heading.

Although we have found these contrasting videos to be essential in providing a clear picture of transformative practice, there are some pitfalls that need to be avoided when they are included in a training design. It is important, for example, that trainees be given clear instructions on what to watch for while they are observing the videos. We have found it useful to have subgroups of trainees watch for (and take notes on) different aspects of the interaction or process as the videos are played, so that the observations can be focused on specific elements of the parties' or mediator's interaction. The discussion afterwards can then be built on all of the different observations from the subgroups. Some useful observation questions for trainees to focus on while they are watching the problem solving videos are:

- How does the parties' interaction change or not change during the mediation?
- Would the parties be able to deal with this or other conflicts more constructively after being involved in the mediation?
- In what ways is the second (subtly directive) mediator's behaviors similar to and different from the first (explicitly directive) mediator's behaviors?
- What forms of directiveness do you see in the mediator's behavior? How do the parties react to the directiveness?

Useful questions to pose for trainees while they are watching the transformative approach include:

- How are this mediator's behaviors different from and similar to the mediation in the prior two videos?
- How do the parties' react to the mediator's approach?
- What specific segments in the interaction illustrate moments where either party moved from a state of relative weakness to greater strength or from being closed to being more open to the other's point of view?
- What specific nonverbal cues does the mediator use that are consistent with the goals of transformative practice?
- Would the parties be able to deal with this or other conflicts more constructively after being involved in the mediation?

Besides focusing trainees' attention on specific elements of the video-taped role plays while they are watching them, it is also useful to go back and discuss specific moments in the interaction after the tape is played in full. This re-playing allows trainees to get a closer look at some of the key turning points in the interaction and to focus on exactly how the mediator follows rather than leads the parties through their emerging conflict interaction. Discussion of these individual segments can be handled much the way the critical point role plays are conducted.

Encourage Trainees to Examine the Nature and Sources of Mediator Directiveness

Special emphasis needs to be placed in training on how party empower-ment can be preserved in practice, and on the challenges that this creates for mediators in the moment-to-moment decisions they make about when and how to intervene. **This means that the training should not only demonstrate the value of empowerment, but address how easy it is for mediators to become directive in working with parties.** Mediators should be encouraged to consider the likely sources of their own directive tendencies.

In reaching this goal, it is helpful to involve trainees in exercises that allow them to experience, first hand, the value of empowerment. This means allowing trainees to experience how being encouraged to think clearly about one's own situation or circumstance, without being led by someone else to a solution, can lead to clarity and certainty about the decisions one wants to make. Exercises that involve real-life situations rather than role plays serve this end well because they provide an opportunity for trainees to experience empowerment first hand.

The "Getting Clear" exercise, for instance, allows trainees to assess what makes any particular move by a third party directive and to experience the positive impact of receiving consistent, non-directive responses from a listener, as they talk about a difficult situation they are currently experiencing in their own life. This exercise works at both an experiential and a conceptual level. From the point of view of the person being listened to, it brings home a clear sense that significant insights can be obtained about one's own problems or situations by interacting with someone who is intentionally trying to be non-directive. Trainees experience, in other words, the value of an interaction process that is built on the concept of empowerment.

From the point of view of the person who is trying to be helpful and at the same time remain non-directive, it allows trainees to experience how strong their own directive instincts might be and to determine, for themselves, how much they need to self-monitor as they practice. In conducting this exercise we have found that trainees have a great deal of difficulty withholding an impulse to tell the person they are listening to what will work, or to give the other person a situation from their own life that can lead them where they think they should end up in dealing with the problem they have been describing. This tendency is quite revealing to trainees – it points to their own strong desire to "solve" things for someone else. When the exercise is discussed and trainees see how much value people gain from being allowed to think through a problem with someone else, without directive intervention, they are more inclined to want to suppress any directive tendencies they might have.

One useful insight that emerges from the discussion of an exercise like this is that defining directiveness in any absolute terms is impossible. **Directiveness is not identifiable in the construction of any given statement or message a mediator might send but rather is determined by**

how the other person takes the comment. Any given behavior or statement by a mediator may or may not be perceived as directive, depending on
how the disputants are likely to hear it. There are a large number of contex-
tual factors that influence how any given comment by a mediator is likely to
be taken. As a result, mediators need to monitor how willing parties are to
take a "suggestion" as a "directive", or how willing they are to interpret a
mediator's "silence" as "criticism". Attempting to remain non-directive
means constantly monitoring context and trying to understand how disputants are interpreting the mediator's behavior. Without careful reading of
each disputant and the immediate context of any comment, mediators cannot
easily assess how any given comment will be taken. **It is only by constantly monitoring that one can remain consistently non-directive.**

In thinking through mediator directiveness with trainees, it is useful to
discuss the range of sources that give rise to the impulse to "lead" rather than
"follow" the parties. This discussion can include consideration of the way in
which social class and social privilege in our society spawn a sense that, as
mediators, we are better able to address issues than the parties themselves. It
can also highlight the way in which professional backgrounds and training —
in the helping and legal professions in particular - can promote directive or
strong-handed approaches to mediation. These professional orientations are
often geared towards "fixing" problems and issues for clients. Finally, these
discussions can include sources of directiveness that are tied to the institu-
tional pressures mediators feel to reach settlements quickly. In some
organizational or court settings mediators can feel pressure to become over-
ly focused on outcomes, with little concern for the disputants' roles in
building those outcomes or the potential shifts in conflict interaction that can
occur among the parties. In discussing these various sources of directiveness,
trainees bring them into fuller awareness and can, as a result, be on guard for
their effects within their own practice.

Rely on Models of the Process that Reflect a Focus on Empowerment and Recognition

Learning how to mediate is often challenging because of the sense of
unpredictability that often governs conflict interaction. It is easy for beginning mediators to feel lost as a session is unfolding. They may feel unsure
about what is happening at the moment, and not be able to integrate what is
going on into some larger sense of how the session as a whole is developing.
For this reason, it is often useful for trainees to see models of the mediation
process — diagrams or visual representations that capture key process elements and interconnections among them.

Most of the existing models of mediation process do not reflect and picture an approach to practice that focuses on empowerment and recognition (Antes et al., 1999; Della Noce, this volume). This is because most of the models are stage models that are based heavily on a problem-solving vision of practice. These stage models depict mediation as a linear process. They imply a sequence of steps that move inexorably forward without cycling or retracing the conflict interaction. They also point mediators toward settlement as the inevitable and/or only outcome of the process. These two characteristics of the stage models, in combination, provide mediators with a picture of practice that easily encourages directive practice — they depict the process of mediation in a way that encourages mediators to lead rather than follow parties through the process.

Although most existing models are generally not useful in conveying a sense of transformative practice, trainees still need some clear visual model of the process to map and guide their intervention work. They need a structure that they can hold on to as they walk through a mediation session. The models that have been developed for transformative practice take into account the evolving, circular interplay of empowerment and recognition that lies at the heart of a transformative process. These models depict party decision-making as the activity at the center of a process that cycles between opportunities for empowerment and recognition. They demonstrate the way in which the willingness for someone to extend recognition to another is often built on some level of empowerment, and the ability to gain clarity about one's true choices, options or resources, is often built upon some level of recognition and acknowledgment of the other. Most importantly, the circular nature of these models conveys an accurate sense that empowerment and recognition doe not happen all at once. Rather, empowerment and recognition occur in small, inter-connected increments over the course of a session. **These models are used both in beginning and advanced trainings to convey a general sense of how a session is likely to unfold, reinforcing the micro-emphasis while still providing an overview of the process as a whole.**

Address Issues about the Viability of Transformative Practice Across Dispute Settings

One of the common myths about transformative mediation is that it is an approach to intervention that can only be practiced in certain dispute contexts. Specifically, the claim is often made that this framework is only appropriate in disputes where ongoing relationships exist between the parties, or when "relationship concerns" are central to the dispute. This is a myth that most often stems from not seeing the difference between a relational and a relationship approach to practice.

A relational framework is a view of conflict interaction that centers on processes of empowerment and recognition –- the transformative vision of productive conflict interaction. A relationship view, on the other hand, is an approach to practice that attempts to alter relationships or have parties achieve reconciliation, even if the parties are not ready or willing to move in this direction. In this approach to practice, mediators frequently feel that a mediation is not successful unless the parties "get to the underlying issues" — the concerns that the mediator assumes lay beneath what the parties are willing or able to talk about. This is a highly directive form of practice that violates the underlying emphasis on empowerment in the transformative framework. In transformative practice, people are allowed to address any issues they want to address, including all relationship issues, but only if they themselves turn their interaction toward those issues. The mediator works with, but does not in any way force, parties to deal with issues that they are not willing or able to address, even if it means that the parties choose not to reconcile or if they leave important aspects of their relationship unresolved.

The difference between a relational and a relationship view of practice needs to be addressed in training to help clarify the goals of transformative mediation. It is important to raise this issue during the training so that mediators are not left with a mistaken impression about the relevance of this approach across dispute settings. All parties who are engaged in conflict interaction — even if it is only for the length of the mediation session itself - are involved in interaction that can be viewed and worked with from the standpoint of empowerment and recognition. This misunderstanding can be addressed by discussing how empowerment and recognition are at the heart of all conflict interaction, regardless of whether the parties have an ongoing relationship beyond the mediation. Productive conflict interaction, among parties who interact for any length of time, requires simultaneous movement from weakness to strength and from self-absorption to openness and responsiveness to the other. Given this explicit view of conflict, the approach to practice is appropriate for any conflict arena. Even when an insurance adjuster and claimant or a business proprietor and customer come to mediation, they are engaged in interactions that raise issues of empowerment and recognition. The transformative model is as relevant here as it is in disputes between divorcing couples or neighbors.

This point can be made in training not only through explicit discussion, but by including a diverse set of role plays and video demonstrations (of both critical points as well as longer segments of mediation) that depict the process in a wide variety of dispute settings. **Depicting transformative practice in business, labor-management and policy disputes as well as community, neighbor, victim-offender, family and divorce mediations clarifies the way in which empowerment and recognition occur across both "relationship" and "non-relationship" settings.** It demonstrates the applicability of the framework in all of these contexts. And, it helps to clarify the way all conflict interaction can be viewed from the standpoint of empowerment and recognition.

Design and Conduct Mediation Training that is Isomorphic with the Underlying Values of the Transformative Framework

In developing both introductory and advanced trainings in transformative practice, we have tried to make sure that the format and style of the training are consistent with the underlying values of the mediation model being taught. **We have tried, in other words, to keep the training isomorphic with the ideology about human nature and human interaction that drives transformative practice itself .**

This means that we try to design and deliver trainings that foster and are built upon transformative interaction - processes of empowerment and recognition for both trainer and trainees. Some of the ways in which this unfolds in practice include:

- being transparent about the goals of each exercise in the training;
- articulating as clearly as possible the value commitments that the training is based on and encouraging trainees to compare it with other frameworks;
- giving trainees options for participation at various points in the training;
- not asking trainees to participate in exercises that are deceptive or have hidden agendas;
- allowing trainees to learn about conflict from the differences and conflicts that arise among trainers and trainees or among trainees;
- acknowledging and being receptive to the struggle trainees might have in moving from one established approach to practice to another.

It is important to recognize that in an approach to training centered on transformative values, an emphasis is placed on empowerment for both the trainer and trainees. This means, on the one hand, that trainees are encouraged to participate fully during all parts of the training, to react and disagree with ideas that are being offered by trainers, and to choose whether they want to adopt the approach to practice being taught. It also means that trainers need to provide themselves with adequate time and resources to teach and fully clarify the framework – to teach the "content" of the training. This may mean offering lectures, showing fairly lengthy portions of video examples of practice and allowing for extensive question and answer periods during the training. It is only when the ideas are clearly and thoroughly presented and discussed that trainees are able to understand the material and make decisions for themselves about their ability or desire to practice within the framework being presented. **It is through empowerment of the trainer that the trainee can be fully empowered.**

When the need for trainer empowerment is neglected, it frequently leads to a view of training in which the entire emphasis is on trainee involvement and participation, often at the expense of clarity on content. Highly elicitive models of training are useful and can give a great deal of respect to the trainees. However, the downside of these approaches is that they can neglect the need for adequate clarity on content from the trainers. This often leads to frustration for some trainees who value the high level of participation but remain confused at the end of a training about the ideas being taught. Our experience has been that for many mediators (especially those who are already practicing) the relational framework is a new way of thinking — something that is not easily elicited because prior training or professional backgrounds have shaped very different ways of thinking about practice. Without adequate contributions by the trainers, the key elements and nature of transformative practice is easily missed.

Finding a balance between trainer and trainee empowerment often leads to unexpected training designs that can be difficult for some to see at first as effective training pedagogy. In designing one of the advanced trainings for a specific client, for example, we met considerable resistance when we planned to show three ½ hour video segments depicting three different approaches to practice in the same mediation case. The concern was that it was poor training technique — people would be bored, would "tune out" - and thus not engage with or learn the ideas being presented. When we have used these videotapes in training, however, our experience has not borne out these concerns. People watch the videos with rapt attention, as they follow instructions in looking for specific elements in the mediations. They see differences in practice that are nearly impossible to express in words. Trainees who had heard about transformative practice but were unclear about what it involved quickly became clear about what the practice looks like and how it is different from other approaches. As trainers, we were confident that the trainees truly understood the approach after watching and discussing the videos. They were able to make informed decisions about whether it is an approach to practice they wanted to try to master in the remaining portions of the training.

Using the Training Principles

These training themes are not intended to be "hard and fast" rules for developing the skills of transformative practice. There are many possible ways that the specific elements of training can be designed and still be consistent with the underlying goals and accomplishments of transformative practice. **There is not one model, but many models of training for this framework.** It is useful, however, to have a set of clear and concise principles in mind as any training activity is designed and delivered. It is very easy for trainers to lose focus, to begin forgetting what any particular training activity is intended to accomplish. When this happens, the training can easily go off track — trainees may enjoy the activities they are asked to participate in but not see the connection between the activities and the goals of the training as a whole. Keeping these principles in mind and making them clear to the trainees themselves, is important to the overall success of the training.

Our experience has been that focusing on the underlying purpose behind practice is essential in allowing trainees to grasp how to use any skills that are taught in mediation training. Most of the training themes we have discussed help in one way or another to convey this purpose behind practice. These principles encourage careful consideration of underlying premises about conflict and human nature. They promote the use of exercises, which allow trainees to experience and reflect upon the likely "outcomes" of a process they are going to be asked to enact as a mediator. And they ask trainers to model, in the training itself, the values that underlie the mediation process. At all of these levels, these principles are helpful in bringing across not simply what mediators do, but why.

BIBLIOGRAPHY

Antes, J. R., Bryant. S. A., & Hendrikson, L. H. (1996). *About face: The relationship between mediator facework and mediation outcome.* Unpublished manuscript.

Antes, J. R., Hudson, D. T., Jorgensen, E. O., & Moen, J. K. (1999). Is a stage model of mediation necessary? *Mediation Quarterly,* 16 (3), 287-301.

Antes, J.R., & Saul, J. (1999, October). *Staying on track with transformative practice: How do we know if mediators have internalized the framework?* Presented at the Hamline University Symposium on Advanced Issues in Conflict Resolution, "Moving to the Next Level in Transformative Mediation: Practice, Research and Policy," St. Paul, MN.

Benjamin, R. D. (1998). Ethical and professional issues in transformative mediation. *Mediation News,* 17 (1), 6-7. Lexington, MA: Academy of Family Mediators.

Benyus, J. (1997). *Biomimicry: Innovation inspired by nature.* New York: Morrow.

Bloom, H. (1987). *The closing of the American mind.* New York: Simon and Shuster.

Bohm, D. (1980). *Wholeness and the implicate order.* London: Ark Paperbacks.

Brookfield, S. (1991). *Understanding and facilitating adult learning.* San Francisco: Jossey-Bass.

Broome, B. J. (1993). Managing differences in conflict resolution: The role of relational empathy. In D. J. D. Sandole & H. van der Merwe (Eds.), *Conflict resolution theory and practice: Integration and application* (pp. 97-111). Manchester: Manchester University Press.

Brown, E. (1988). Divorce mediation in a mental health setting. In J. Folberg & A. Milne (Eds.), *Divorce mediation: Theory and practice* (pp.127-141). New York: Guilford Press.

Burkitt, I. (1999). Relational moves and generative dances. In S. McNamee & K. J. Gergen (Eds.), *Relational responsibility: Resources for sustainable dialogue* (pp. 71-79). Thousand Oaks, CA: Sage.

Bush, R. A. B. (1989). Efficiency and protection, or empowerment and recognition?: The mediator's role and ethical standards in mediation. *Florida Law Review,* 41, 253-286.

Bush, R. A. B. (1996). "What do we need a mediator for?": Mediation's "value-added" for negotiators. *Ohio State Journal of Dispute Resolution,* 12 (1), 1-36.

Bush, R. A. B. & Folger, J. P. (1994). *The promise of mediation: Responding to conflict through empowerment and recognition.* San Francisco: Jossey-Bass.

Bush, R. A. B., Folger, J. P., Della Noce, D. J., & Pope, S. G. (1998). *Advanced mediation skills for postal service mediators.* Washington, D.C.: U.S. Postal Service.

Chasin, R., Herzig, M., Roth, S., Chasin, L., Becker, C., & Stains, R. (1996). From diatribe to dialogue on divisive public issues: Approaches drawn from family therapy. *Mediation Quarterly,* 13 (4), 323-344.

Cobb, S. (1991). Einsteinian practice and Newtonian discourse: An ethical crisis in mediation. *Negotiation Journal,* 7 (1), 87-102.

Cobb, S. (1993). Empowerment and mediation: A narrative perspective. *Negotiation Journal,* 9, 245-259.

Cobb, S. & Rifkin, J. (1991). Practice and paradox: Deconstructing neutrality in mediation. *Law & Social Inquiry,* 16 (1), 35-62.

Cooperrider, D. and Srivasta, S. (1987). Appreciative inquiry in organizational life. In W. Pasmore & R. Woodman (Eds.), *Research in organization change and development* (Vol. 1) (pp. 129-169). Greenwich, CT: JAI Press.

Deck, K., & Rockhill, N. (1997). *Fostering recognition and empowerment: Some tools for trainers.* Presentation at the National Conference on Peacemaking and Conflict Resolution, Pittsburgh, PA.

Deetz, S. & White, W. J. (1999). Relational responsibility or dialogic ethics? A questioning of McNamee and Gergen. In S. McNamee & K. J. Gergen (Eds.), *Relational responsibility: Resources for sustainable dialogue* (pp.111-120). Thousand Oaks, CA: Sage.

Della Noce, D. J. (1997). What is a model for mediation practice? A critical review of Family Mediation: Contemporary Issues. *Mediation Quarterly,* 15 (2), 133-142.

Della Noce, D. J. (1999). Seeing theory in practice: An analysis of empathy in mediation. *Negotiation Journal,* 15 (3), 271-301.

Doherty, W. J. (1998). How therapists threaten marriages. In A. Etzioni (Ed.), *The essential communitarian reader* (pp. 157-166). Lanham, MD: Rowman & Littlefield Publishers.

Duan, C. & Hill, C. E. (1996). The current state of empathy research. *Journal of Counseling Research*, 43 (3), 261-274.

Fairclough, N. (1989). *Language and power.* London: Addison Wesley Longman.

Fairclough, N. (1995). *Critical discourse analysis: The critical study of language.* London: Addison Wesley Longman.

Falk, D. R. & Johnson, D. W. (1977). The effects of perspective-taking and egocentrism on problem-solving in heterogeneous and homogeneous groups. *The Journal of Social Psychology*, 102, 63-72.

Folberg, J. & Milne, A. (Eds.). (1988). *Divorce mediation: Theory and practice.* London: Guilford Press.

Folberg, J. & Taylor, A. (1984). *Mediation: A comprehensive guide to resolving disputes without litigation.* San Francisco: Jossey-Bass.

Folger, J. P. (1996, April). *A transformative approach to mediation: Skills for practice.* Presentation at the University of North Dakota, Grand Forks, ND.

Folger, J. P. & Bush, R. A. B. (1994). Ideology, orientations to conflict, and mediation discourse. In J. P. Folger & T. S. Jones (Eds.), *New directions in mediation: Communication research and perspectives* (pp. 3-25). Thousand Oaks, CA: Sage.

Folger, J. P. & Bush, R. A. B. (1996). Transformative mediation and third party intervention: Ten hallmarks of transformative mediation practice. *Mediation Quarterly*, 13 (4), 263-278.

Folger, J. P. & Jones, T. S. (1994). Epilogue: Toward furthering dialogue between researchers and practitioners. In J. P. Folger & T. S. Jones (Eds.), *New directions in mediation: Communication research and perspectives* (pp. 222-227). Thousand Oaks, CA: Sage.

Freire, Paolo (1973). *Pedagogy of the oppressed.* New York: Seabury.

Gray, B. (1994). The gender-based foundations of negotiation theory. In R. J. Lewicki, B. H. Sheppard & R. Bies (Eds.), *Research on negotiations in organizations* (Vol. 4) (pp. 3-35). Greenwich, CT: JAI Press.

Greenhalgh, L. (1995). Competition in a collaborative context: Toward a new paradigm. In R. J. Bies, R. J. Lewicki, & B. H. Sheppard (Eds.), *Research on negotiation in organizations* (Vol. 5) (pp. 251-270). Greenwich, CT: JAI Press, Inc.

Greenhalgh, L. & Chapman, D. I. (1995). Joint decision making: The inseparability of relationships and negotiation. In R. M. Kramer & D. M. Messick (Eds.), *Negotiation as a social process* (pp.166-185). Thousand Oaks, CA: Sage.

Grillo, T. (1996). Respecting the struggle: Following the parties' lead. *Mediation Quarterly*, 13 (4), 279-286.

Haynes, J. M. (1992). Mediation and therapy: An alternate view. *Mediation Quarterly*, 10 (1), 21-34.

Haynes, J. M. (1994). *The fundamentals of family mediation.* NY: State University of New York Press.

Haynes, J. M. & Haynes, G. L. (1989). *Mediating divorce: Casebook of strategies for successful family negotiations.* San Francisco: Jossey-Bass.

Hekman, S. J. (1995). *Moral voices, moral selves: Carol Gilligan and feminist moral theory.* University Park, PA: The State University of New York Press.

Honeyman, C. (1990). The common core of mediation. *Mediation Quarterly*, 8 (1), 73-82.

Huber, S. K. (in press). Transformative mediation in the workplace. *Alternative Dispute Resolution in Employment.*

Irving, H. H. & Benjamin, M. (1995). *Family mediation: Contemporary issues.* ThousandOaks: Sage.

Jantsch, E. *The self-organizing universe.* Oxford: Pergamon, 1980.

Jones, E. E. & Davis, K. E. (1965). From acts to dispositions: The attribution process in person perception. In L. Berkowitz (Ed.), *Advances in experimental social psychology (Vol. 2).* New York: Academic Press. 1965.

Jones, T. S. (1994). A dialectical reframing of the mediation process. In J. P. Folger & T. S. Jones (Eds.), *New directions in mediation: Communication research and perspectives* (pp. 26-47). Thousand Oaks, CA: Sage.

Kelley, H. H. (1971). *Attribution in social interaction.* Morristown NJ: General Learning Press.

Kelly, J. (1983). Mediation and psychotherapy: Distinguishing the differences. *Mediation Quarterly*, 1 (1), 33-44.

Kelly, J. B. (1995). Power imbalance in divorce and interpersonal mediation. *Mediation Quarterly*, 13 (2), 85-98.

Kemp, K. E. & Smith, W. P. (1994). Information exchange, toughness, and integrative bargaining: The roles of explicit cues and perspective-taking. *The International Journal of Conflict Management,* 5 (1), 5-21.

Knowles, Malcom (1970). *The modern practice of adult education: Andragogy versus pedagogy.* Chicago: Association Press.

Koehn, D. (1998). *Rethinking feminist ethics: Care, trust and empathy.* London: Routledge.

Kolb, D. M. (Ed.). (1994). *When talk works: Profiles of mediators.* San Francisco: Jossey-Bass.

Kolb, D. M. & Putnam, L. L. (1997). Through the looking glass: Negotiation refracted through the lens of gender. In S. Gleason (Ed.), *Workplace dispute resolution: Directions for the 21st century* (pp. 231-257). East Lansing: Michigan State University Press.

Kovach, K. K. (1994). *Mediation: Principles and practice.* St. Paul, MN: West Publishing Co.

Lannaman, J. W. (1999). On being relational in an accountable way: The questions of agency and power. In S. McNamee & K. J. Gergen (Eds.), *Relational responsibility: Resources for sustainable dialogue* (pp. 81-91). Thousand Oaks, CA: Sage.

Lederach, J. P. (1995). *Preparing for peace: Conflict resolution across cultures.* Syracuse, NY: Syracuse University Press.

Mansbridge, J. J. (1983). *Beyond adversary democracy.* Chicago: University of Chicago Press.

Mansbridge, J. J. (1990). The rise and fall of self-interest in the explanation of political life. In J. J. Mansbridge (Ed.), *Beyond self-interest* (pp. 3-22). Chicago: University of Chicago Press.

McNamee, S. & Gergen, K. J. (1999). *Relational responsibility: Resources for sustainable dialogue.* Thousand Oaks, CA: Sage.

Menkel-Meadow, C. (1995). The many ways of mediation: The transformation of traditions, ideologies, paradigms and practices. *Negotiation Journal,* 11 (3), 217-242.

Milne, A. & Folberg, J. (1988). The theory and practice of divorce mediation: An overview. In J. Folberg & A. Milne (Eds.), *Divorce mediation: Theory and practice* (pp. 3-25). New York, NY: Guilford Press.

Mnookin, R. H., Peppet, S. R., & Tulumello, A. S. (1996). The tension between empathy and assertiveness. *Negotiation Journal,* 12 (3), 217-230.

Moore, C. W. (1996). *The mediation process: Practical strategies for resolving conflict.* San Francisco: Jossey-Bass.

Neale, M. A. & Bazerman, M. H. (1983). The role of perspective-taking ability in negotiating under different forms of arbitration. *Industrial and Labor Relations Review,* 36 (3), 378-388.

Olaniran, B. A. (1996). Group process satisfaction and decision quality in computer-mediated communication: An examination of contingent relations. In R. S. Cathcart, L. A. Samovar, & L. D. Henman (Eds.) *Small group communication: Theory & practice* (7th Ed.), (pp.134-146). Madison, WI: Brown & Benchmark Publishers.

Palmer, P. (1998). *The courage to teach.* San Francisco: Jossey-Bass.

Pearce, W. B., & Littlejohn, S.W. (1997). *Moral conflict: When social worlds collide.* Thousand Oaks, CA: Sage.

Peat, F. D. (1998). *Synchronicity: The bridge between matter and mind.* New York: Bantam.

Poole, M.S. & Baldwin, C.L. (1996). Developmental processes in group decision making. In R.Y. Hirokawa & M. S. Poole (Eds.), *Communication and group decisionmaking* (2d Ed.) (pp. 215-241). Thousand Oaks, CA: Sage.

Poole, M. S., Seibold, D. R., & McPhee, R. D. (1996). The structuration of group decisions. In R.Y. Hirokawa & M. S. Poole (Eds.), *Communication and group decisionmaking* (2d Ed.) (pp. 114-146). Thousand Oaks, CA: Sage.

Pope, S. G. (1996). Inviting fortuitous events in mediation: The role of empowerment and recognition. *Mediation Quarterly,* 13 (4), 287-294.

Putnam, L. L. (1994). Challenging the assumptions of traditional approaches to negotiation. *Negotiation Journal,* 10 (3), 337-346.

Rappaport, J. (1987). Terms of empowerment/exemplars of prevention: Toward a theory for community psychology. *American Journal of Community Psychology,* 15, 121-144.

Richardson, D. R., Hammock, G. S., Smith, S. M., Gardner, W., & Signo, M. (1994). Empathy as a cognitive inhibitor of interpersonal aggression. *Aggressive Behavior,* 20, 275-289.

Rilke, R. M. (1962). *Letters to a young poet.* New York: W. W. Norton.

Roberts, B. B. & Thorsheim, H. I. (1987). *Empowering leadership: A brief intro-duction.* Northfield, MN: St. Olaf College.

Rubin, J. Z., Pruitt, D. G., & Kim, S. H. (1994). *Social conflict: Escalation, stale-mate, and settlement* (2d Ed.). New York: McGraw-Hill.

Sessa, V. I. (1996). Using perspective-taking to manage conflict and affect in teams. *Journal of Applied Behavioral Science,* 32 (1), 101-115.

Shailor, J. G. (1994). *Empowerment in dispute mediation: A critical analysis of com-munication.* Westport, CT: Praeger.

Slaikeu, K. A. (1996). *When push comes to shove: A practical guide to mediating dis-putes.* San Francisco: Jossey Bass.

Slaikeu, K. A., Pearson, J., & Thoennes, N. (1988). Divorce mediation behav-iors: A descriptive system and analysis. In J. Folberg & A. Milne, *Divorce mediation: Theory and practice* (pp. 475-495). New York: Guilford Press.

Tannen, D. (1998). *The argument culture: Moving from debate to dialogue.* New York: Random House.

Taylor, A. (1988). A general theory of divorce mediation. In J. Folberg and A. Milne (Eds.), *Divorce mediation: Theory and practice* (pp. 61-82). New York: Guilford Press.

Van Dijk, T. A. (1998). *Ideology: A multidisciplinary study.* London: Sage.

Van Lear, C. A. (1996). Communication process approaches and models: Patterns, cycles and dynamic coordination. In J. H. Watt & C. A. Van Lear, *Dynamic patterns in communication processes* (pp. 35-70). Thousand Oaks, CA: Sage.

Wheatley, M. (1992). *Leadership and the new science: Learning about organization from an orderly universe.* San Francisco, CA: Berrett-Koehler.

Whyte, D. (1994). *The heart aroused: poetry and the preservation of the soul in corpo-rate America.* New York: Doubleday.

Zimmerman, M. A. (1995). Psychological empowerment: Issues and illus-trations. *American Journal of Community Psychology,* 23, 581-599.

ABOUT THE CONTRIBUTORS

James R. Antes, PhD, is Professor of Psychology and Peace Studies at the University of North Dakota and former director of the UND Conflict Resolution Center. He has extensive experience in the field of conflict resolution as a mediator, workshop leader, and consultant, and has numerous publications and presentations at professional conferences on various aspects of conflict resolution.

Robert A. Baruch Bush, JD, is the Rains Distinguished Professor of Alternative Dispute Resolution (ADR) and Law at Hofstra Law School, Hempstead, NY. Author of numerous articles and frequent presenter, he is co-author, with Dr. Joseph Folger, of *The Promise of Mediation* (1994). He has served as a consultant on dispute resolution to courts, school systems, foundations and government agencies, including the United States Postal Service REDRESS™ Mediation Program.

Susan Beal, MA, has been a mediator since 1992, with experience in community, family, school, and multi-party mediation and facilitation. She earned an MA in Conflict Resolution in 1995 from Antioch University. While Susan enjoys mediating, she finds greatest satisfaction in training others in the development of their own listening, communication and conflict resolution skills. Currently, Susan is observing the mediation world from the sidelines while indulging another passion: editing and publishing a small alternative newspaper in her home state of Vermont.

Paul Charbonneau, MA, is an Associate of the Institute for the Study of Conflict Transformation in New York and a principal in the dispute resolution firm, Charbonneau & Galloway of Rockport and Brunswick, Maine. Mr. Charbonneau has been a mediator since 1984 and served for nearly six years as Director of the Maine State Court Mediation Service, a statewide court-connected mediation program. He is adjunct faculty for mediation and conflict management studies at the University of Maine, the University of Southern Maine, and teaches mediation ethics at Woodbury College in Montpelier, Vermont. Mr. Charbonneau received his undergraduate degree in Philosophy from the University of Ottawa and his Masters degree in Liberal Studies from the University of Maine.

Dorothy J. Della Noce, JD, has been active in the mediation field for more than a decade, providing mediation services and training, serving in leadership roles in various state and national organizations, and participating in numerous initiatives to move theory into practice. She is a 1979 graduate of LaSalle College in Philadelphia, and she received her JD from Western New England School of Law in 1983. She is currently a doctoral candidate in Communication Sciences at Temple University, where she was awarded a University Fellowship. She is completing her dissertation research on the discourse practices of mediators.

Joseph P. Folger, PhD, is a Professor of Communication at Temple University in Philadelphia. He has been the program chair for the National Conference on Peacemaking and Conflict Resolution and has helped to establish several major conflict intervention programs. He is currently a senior consultant with Communication Research Associates where he conducts communication skills training, coaching and conflict intervention. Dr. Folger has published extensively in the area of communication, conflict and mediation. His recent books include the award-winning volumes *Working Through Conflict: Strategies for Relationships, Groups and Organizations, 3rd Edition* (with S. Poole and R. K. Stutman) and *The Promise of Mediation* (with Robert A. B. Bush). He has also published numerous research articles as well as the edited volume, *New Directions in Mediation* (with T. S. Jones).

Linda Hendrikson, MA, is a Services Coordinator at the University of North Dakota's Conflict Resolution Center. Linda coordinates the efforts of a diverse group of professionals to provide a wide range of conflict management and educational services to the University and the region. She serves as a mediator, group facilitator, trainer, consultant, and as a mentor to new mediators. She has an MA in Counseling from the University of North Dakota.

Donna Turner Hudson, MA, is a mediator, trainer and consultant in private practice in Grand Forks, North Dakota. She holds a master's degree in Educational Counseling and Psychology from the University of Missouri-Columbia and over ten years experience in the field of conflict management. She is a charter member and former senior services coordinator for the University of North Dakota's Conflict Resolution Center.

Erling Jorgensen is a doctoral candidate in the Department of Counseling at the University of North Dakota. He is a former intern at UND's Conflict Resolution Center with experiences as a mediator, group facilitator, and workshop leader. His doctoral research investigates parties' perceptions of significant moments during mediation.

Janet Kelly Moen, PhD, is Professor of Sociology and Peace Studies at the University of North Dakota. She is a charter member of the Conflict Resolution Center and Faculty Coordinator for the Center for Peace Studies at the University. She is presently doing research in the application of principles of transformative mediation in international relations.

Sally Ganong Pope, MEd, JD, is a private mediation practitioner in New York City. She has taught mediation as an Adjunct Professor at Benjamin N. Cardozo School of Law, Brooklyn Law School and Pepperdine Law School. She is a former President of the Academy of Family Mediators and was part of the mediation training design team for the US Postal Service's REDRESS™ Program.

Judith A. Saul is founder and Executive Director of the Community Dispute Resolution Center in Ithaca, New York, serving three counties and offering a range of dispute resolution and training services to people of all ages, schools, businesses, organizations and government. She is a leader in the community mediation field, both state-wide and nationally and serves on the Alternative Dispute Resolution Advisory Committee for New York's Unified Court System and on an American Bar Association Committee that is drafting a Model Mediation Statute. She has served as co-chair of the Board of the National Association for Community Mediation.

Robert R. Stains, Jr., MEd, LMFT, is Director of Training of the Public Conversations Project and is on the faculty of the Family Institute of Cambridge. At PCP he co-designs and co-facilitates constructive conversations on such controversial issues as abortion and sexual orientation. He also co-developed and co-presents PCP's "Power of Dialogue" and "Inquiry as Intervention" workshops and is a frequent presenter at national and international conferences. He contributed to Bush and Folger's Training Design Consultation and was a core trainer of mediators for the US Postal Service's REDRESS™ program. He provides training and consultation to national and international organizations on creating openings for constructive conversation in the midst of conflict and mediates for the REDRESS™ program. He maintains a private mediation, counseling and training practice in Beverly, MA.